Individuality and Primal Unity: Ego's Struggle for Dominance in Today's World

by Jim Willis

Volume I: Ego and Earth Magic
(*Merlin the Magician: A Mystery for the Ages*)

Volume II: Ego and the Hero
(*Robin Hood: Victory Through Defiance*)

Volume III: Ego and Innocence
(*Little Snow-White: A Road Map for Our Time*)

Individuality and Primal Unity: Ego's Struggle for Dominance in Today's World - Volume I: Ego and Earth Magic (Merlin the Magician: A Mystery for the Ages)
© 2021 Jim Willis
ISBN: 978-1-989940-37-2
Dimensionfold Publishing

Preface

At some point in the distant past, a remote, ancient ancestor began to think in terms of the word "I." He or she became the first to understand the concept of individuality—the idea that "I" am separate and distinct from "You," and harbor different needs and desires. In that moment, *Ego* was born and humankind was metaphorically cast out of Eden. The struggle for existence, now understood in terms of a struggle for individual survival, began. No longer was identity found in species recognition. The "One" became the "Many." Unity was fractured. Henceforth the individual would reign supreme. "Look out for #1" became a human mantra and the quest for individual power began.

It continues to this day. Ego didn't necessarily lose the ability to feel empathy and compassion, but from the very beginning its primary instincts were for personal protection, survival, and growth. This has led to such concepts as the divine right of kings, class warfare, political dominance, top-heavy economic control over the means of industrial production, and monetary benefits for the few as opposed to the many.

Especially in these days of social media, every morning it has become standard procedure for many people to stare into the allegorical mirror of their computer screen, affirm their social status based on the number of responses they generated overnight, and ask, "Who is the fairest of them all?" It would appear as though Snow-White's evil stepmother has been reincarnated and lives on in modern society. Increasingly, we find ourselves living in Ego's home country, a land called Narcissism.

How do we resist such an insidious enemy? As always, those who came before left us clues to follow. Their wisdom forms the basis of this trilogy.

Those who created the old, familiar myths, legends, and fireside tales were well aware of the dangers of Ego. They might not have understood the struggle in modern, psychological terms. But they were intuitive enough to compose stories about it. In these imaginative tales they pitted Ego against the healing magic of Earth Energy, the ancestral Eden from whence Ego had sprung.

Eventually, the civilized "Ego of the City" sought to destroy its wild and untamed predecessor who still lived out in the natural world. It is not by accident that the biblical story begins in a Genesis garden, and ends in a Revelation city. It is revealing when Hebrew mythology records that right after the first murder was perpetrated because of a bruised ego, the murderer, Cain, went out and built a city east of Eden. Ever since, the metaphorical story of civilization is the story of the power struggle between cities. Industrial civilization, not the army, destroyed the American Indians. Today's headlines remind us again and again that the technology of development is a two-edged sword. Urban blight is a principal enemy of nature's resources. These stories mark the progress of Ego's conquests.

We will explore this subject by means of an in-depth analysis of three ancient tales. Each story will be developed in a separate book which can stand alone on its own, but will be part of a trilogy that encompasses the three stages of Ego's rise to dominance.

Part I: Ego and Earth Magic (*Merlin the Magician: A Mystery for the Ages*)

In the Arthurian legends, Merlin the Magician is pitted against dark energies summoned by Ego, who seeks to destroy the source of ancient Earth Magic. At the end,

Ego appears to be victorious. Merlin is presented as the last of the old ones to be associated with natural magic, and is entombed in a crystal cave, deep in the bowels of the earth.

But just as in the Christ story, the Arthurian tale of the *Once and Future King*, the American Indian Tecumseh legends, and the Tolkien Ring Cycle, there is the promise of a return. Merlin will one day awake to be reunited with Arthur. The union of Earth Magic and spiritual Camelot will be spread abroad "on earth, as it is in heaven."

Until then, however, with ancient Earth Magic seemingly destroyed, or at least imprisoned, Ego is free to strike out at those humans who still follow the old, earth-based, natural ways.

Part II: Ego and the Hero (*Robin Hood: Victory Through Defiance*)

The Hero, Robin Hood, is a nature man who is at home in the wild forests of Sherwood. He defies the ego-centric, power-hungry sheriff of Nottingham, who remains ensconced in his fortified urban castle. In the end, the Hero teaches us to be victorious by defying Ego's claims on personal freedom and individual choice. Robin Hood refuses walls and the loss of independence. His final victory is assured with the return of King Richard, and his marriage to Marian reunites nature and civilization into one spiritual landscape.

Part III: Ego and Innocence (*Little Snow-White: A Road Map for Our Time*)

In the story of *Little Snow-White*, Queen Ego, secure in her castle, seeks to destroy Snow-White, who represents Intuitive Innocence. Snow-White lives in the wild forest "across the seven mountains" with the seven dwarfs. In the end, Innocence triumphs over Ego through her interaction with earth energies. As in the story of Robin Hood, once victory is assured, her marriage to the prince from a faraway, mysterious land, unites the physical and the spiritual aspects of life in our perception realm. (Spoiler alert: Awakening Snow-White with a kiss is a Disney abomination. In the original version, she awakens through interaction with Earth Energy!)

In the first tale, Earth Magic is seemingly neutralized and imprisoned in the crystal cave of the earth. This is a picture of 21st century life. Civilization has brought about a feeling of deadness when it comes to the natural world. We have separated ourselves from the very Earth Mother who gave us birth. Ego can never-the-less be defeated by energies and forces inherent in the natural world. Therein lies our hope and our salvation. Earth Energy slumbers, but is not defeated. Not yet.

In the next two stories we explore the current status of Ego in today's world. It battles both the Hero and the Innocent, but Earth Magic still comes to the aid of the deserving if we are attuned to its beckoning call.

All three stories reach their climax when hope arrives in the guise of "Royalty" from outside, a reference to spiritual help that is always available to those who are in touch with nature. In the case of Merlin, spiritual aid comes from Arthur the King. Robin Hood welcomes the return of King Richard. Snow-White is joined by the mysterious prince. None of these visitors arrives to "save the day." Rather, they make their entrance after the battle is already won. Their presence may have been subtle and understated, but their ancient magic and power was none the less available.

So it is that in our civilized world, invented and dominated by materialistic Ego, selfish individuality often appears to be victorious, while archaic Earth Magic seems imprisoned in a tomb. But in the end, spiritual energies from the natural world, which is a manifestation of the Source of All That Is, offers the hope of triumph over seemingly impossible odds.

Individualistic Ego's demise, we are assured, is certain, and the unity of Eden will again be restored when spirituality arrives in the flesh to participate in the final victory.

In the end, this is a trilogy of hope.

Merlin the Magician:
A Mystery for the Ages

Jim Willis

Dedication

This book is dedicated to two mentors
whom I have never met:

Mary Stewart, who first made Merlin come alive for me,
and
Robert Bly, who taught me how to understand his story.

I owe you both a great debt!

Table of Contents

Introduction	1
Chapter 1: Merlin and the Legend	19
Chapter 2: Merlin and Earth Magic	43
Chapter 3: Merlin and the Dragon	65
Chapter 4: Merlin and the Giant's Dance	89
Chapter 5: Merlin and the Child	115
Chapter 6: Merlin and the Sword	147
Chapter 7: Merlin and Wilderness Wisdom	173
Chapter 8: Merlin and the City	185
Chapter 9: Merlin and the Crystal Cave	207
Conclusion: The Return of Merlin	225
Further Reading	237
About the Author	241

Introduction

A poet, an artist, and a musician walk into a bar. There they engage in an esoteric, enlightening discussion that offers them all a transcendent vision of the human condition. For a moment, they all see the world, and humanity's place in it, in a new way that seems somehow transforming. Not having the prosaic language to quite put their insight into words, they all resort to their own particular medium. The poet writes a poem. The artist paints a picture. The musician composes a song. The poem, the picture, and the song are totally different from one another, but they all produce similar feelings in their respective audiences because they are all based on the same, shared, transformative theme. They hope to convey an important insight.

In the same way, when we approach a subject such as lore about Merlin the Magician, we are engaging an old, old story that has been cast in poetry, history, music, art, and literature. Through it all is woven a story that has stood the test of time.

Is it based on a historical figure? Maybe. But

probably not.

Is Merlin a composite, based on several historical figures who lived in different geographical locations and different historical times? Maybe. But probably not.

Are his actions based on real, historical events? Maybe. But probably not.

Could he really produce magic simply by being Merlin? Maybe. But probably not.

Over the course of time Merlin's importance has grown far beyond the motivations, methods, and deeds of any one man. It's his *story* that is of eternal importance, not the historical relevance of his deeds.

Think of it this way. Sometimes religion is not enough. We need more. Sometimes scientific explanations are insufficient. We need more. Sometimes mythological relevance doesn't quite satisfy. We need more. Sometimes psychological motivation doesn't do it for us. We need more. Sometimes philosophical discussion falls short. We need more.

Merlin has become the "more."

We live in a maddeningly literal age. We somehow

have accepted the idea that if a character isn't historical, he or she wasn't "real." We have come to believe that if a historical Buddha didn't live in India 2,500 years ago, Buddhism is a false intellectual structure. If it could be proved that a historical Jesus didn't walk the paths of ancient Galilee, Christianity would cease to be deemed viable. If Lao Tzu wasn't a real person, Daoism is worthless. If Arthur and Merlin are not based on actual people, Arthurian studies are a waste of time.

Nothing could be further from the truth. Many people have no idea any other world view is possible. But that's what they get when they choose to follow only fact-driven, scientifically-minded, intellectually-reasoned, ego-induced thought structures that claim reality can't be understood when couched in a story that is "just a myth."

They are wrong. Merlin stands in direct opposition to that way of thinking. He is an antidote to the sickness of ego-based materialism. His story is a plea for a return to the sanity of magic.

Let me explain what I mean by such a blatant statement. Our current predominate world view is composed of a relatively modern way of understanding reality. We think that if we can't see it, taste it, smell it, feel it, hear it, or otherwise measure it, it doesn't exist. That belief is called materialism. But things weren't always subject to such a boring, so-called adult-focused, scientifically determined, fact-based approach to life. There are many things that are very real but not material at root.

Consider the Santa Claus myth, for instance. As children, many of us were fortunate enough to be raised by astute parents who seemingly believed in magic. We used to exhibit a blind belief in a man with a red suit and white beard who came down the chimney to bring us presents on Christmas Eve. We were convinced he knew when we were good or bad, and kept a record, so we tried hard to "be good, for goodness' sake."

We interpreted the Christmas myth in a very literal sense. There was a real workshop at the North Pole, a real Rudolph, a real sleigh, and a real Santa. A large cultural conspiracy—consisting of television shows, songs, an adult population that participated in the ruse, peer pressure at school, and our social network—convinced us the myth was true. So we believed, even if each passing year found us asking more questions.

This was very common, and goes back quite a way. As far back as 1897, Francis Church, writing for *The New York Sun* newspaper, felt moved to respond to a question from a young reader named Virginia O'Hanlon. "Please tell me the truth," Miss O'Hanlon asked. "My father says that if it's printed in the *Sun*, it's true. Is there a Santa Claus?"

Church's answer was the now famous clarion call, "Yes, Virginia, there is a Santa Claus."

He wasn't lying to a gullible kid. There really *is* a Santa Claus. It's just that he is something different from a historical, flesh-and-blood being. There may not be a workshop at the North Pole. But that doesn't mean the myth is a lie. Try calling it the Spirit of Christmas or some such thing. Then you can say wholeheartedly, "Yes, Virginia, there is a Santa Claus!" The season takes on new meaning. The Christmas tradition becomes significant not for what it tells us about Santa Claus, but for what it tells us about the nature of humanity—about love, compassion, wonder, and transcendent magic. The importance lies in the truth behind the story—the reality to which the story points.

Santa *is* alive and well. He wears the guise of loving parents and friends. He brings joy and fun to the drab days of the winter solstice, when nights are long, and cold sets in. He is found to be alive and well in every person who gets into the Christmas spirit.

If we can open our minds to that truth, we will discover greater magic than can possibly be contained in any historical personage. When Santa is freed from the shackles of a single historical character, and no longer limited to scientific fact, he can fulfill the idea of "more." Explanations are then insufficient. Only the work of poets, artists, and musicians will do.

When this truth breaks through and becomes apparent, you don't say, "I understand." You say, "Ah ha!" You get it. You may not be able to put it into words, but you glimpse a transcendent reality beyond the ability of language to adequately express.

This is the power of myth. It transports us to the land of "more." It explains the power of Merlin the Magician.

It also reveals the paucity of mental thought processes common to many people who were born and raised in our intellectual age. You can't condense transcendent reality to a few characters that will fit on a smart phone screen. You can't dissect such things as love and compassion, and look at them under a microscope. Yet people are willing to die for them. Who would be willing to die for something that doesn't exist?

Existential truth is not always conducive to bumper-sticker-sized spaces. It takes patience, nuance, and understanding to move beyond surface reality into the mists of magic, the description of which can't be limited to 280 characters. Sadly however, magical attributes seem to have atrophied in today's busy, techno-centered, science-based world.

They can, however, be coaxed out of the crystal cave in which we have imprisoned them. Merlin didn't live "back then." He didn't live "over there." He lives in us, and our inner Merlin can yet be freed from its entombment. All it takes is a little imagination and intention on our part. Then the magic can be released.

All this is to say that in the following pages we're not going to spend much time arguing that a real, historical character named Merlin once existed. That quest is fun, and has consumed a lot of paper and TV documentary time. Instead, we're going to examine the stories that have grown up around his legend. We're going to argue that those stories are more important that his physical life, if, indeed, he ever lived one. Merlin lore grew because the name Merlin became the focus for a greater reality. He is, and always has been since his inception, a means to express an inner truth that extends above and beyond language. The very word "magic" is so incrusted with linguistic baggage that it is almost useless these days.

A few hundred years ago a horseless carriage was considered magical. The act of turning on a battery-powered flashlight might have got you burned at the stake. If you insisted people could walk on the moon, you would have been laughed out of your village.

Never the less, stories about all those things were once told and enjoyed. Magic carpets, saying the "magic word," and casting magic spells which provided entrance to magical kingdoms, were common. All such notions would have been called silly if you stuck to the facts of science and a superficial, materialistic world view.

Yet people did talk about them, as long as they were presented in fantastic stories and fictional fireside tales. So who is to say that Merlin lore won't someday prove to present a greater reality than we experience today—a reality that one day might be taken for granted? And even if the outward magical mechanics don't come to pass, the truths to which the stories point can help in many ways to illuminate the darkness of our humdrum lives by releasing the magic that still dwells within each one of us, buried deep beneath the detritus of 21st century materialism.

Merlin lore is mythological lore, and mythology shows us how to navigate the perils of everyday, ego-driven activity. It tells us who we are and how we got here. It points to the paths wise men and women have already taken, and guides us into the experience of full human potentiality.

To see how and why this lore accumulated we have to go back to the beginning.

A Quick History of the Merlin Tradition

Somewhere in the ninth century, in a time period purported to be "the fourth year of the reign of King Mermenus, also called Merfyn Frych ap Gwiad, king of Gwynedd," a Welsh scholar who called himself Nennius wrote a supposed history called *Historia Brittonum*, or "The History of the Britons." He claimed that his book revealed the history of the British people. In other words, he said he was writing about his culture's identity, and where they came from.

Many scholars have since decided the work was a forgery, but in the long run, it doesn't matter. The point is that someone, at some time, was asking the questions, "Who are we and how did we get here?"

The date for *Historia Brittonum* is determined from the fact that in Chapter 4, Nennius says that "from the Passion of Christ, 796 years have passed, but from his Incarnation are 831 years." That would make Jesus 35 years old when he died. So most historians who take Nennius seriously assume he wrote his book around 828 or so, leaving a few years for the actual writing before the book started to circulate.

He relates quite a tale, and presents a history that would make the most conservative British citizen proud. Britain, according to Nennius, was first settled by people who escaped the battle of Troy, famous for such god-like characters as Helen, whose "face launched a thousand ships," Achilles, whose only weakness was located in his heal, Odysseus, of the famed voyage following the battle, Ajax, and Hector, to say nothing of the Trojan Horse that figured so prominently in the defeat of the impregnable city.

According to Nennius, one of the founders of Britain was Brutus, descended from Aeneas, whose father was a first cousin of none other than King Priam of Troy. It is from the name Brutus that the word "Briton" is derived. This is the book that first mentions the young Arthur, about whom we will have much to say later. He is called a *deux bellorum*, a "war leader," who famously fought twelve battles which united Britain during perilous times.

The reason Nennius' *Historia Brittonum* is so important is because Geoffrey of Monmouth used it as his primary source when he wrote his classic *Historia regum Britanniae,* the "History of the Kings of Britain," sometime between 1135 and 1138—the book that introduced the first version of the now familiar stories about Merlin Ambrosius, Uther Pendragon, and King Arthur. Geoffrey developed the Merlin figure further in his *Vita Merlini*, the "Life of Merlin." This is the work that began the tradition of Merlin as a magician, a natural wild man of the forests, who possessed the gift of divination and the ability to work all manner of fantastic things just by being Merlin.

By the time of the 13th century this image had caught on. Robert de Borron wrote a romance called *Merlin,* which turned an old Druid into a bit of a Christian prophet of the Holy Grail, the cup of the last supper.

Perhaps this was too big a transition to accept, because an extensive work called the *Vulgate Cycle* returned to an exploration of Merlin's dark side. But by the end of the cycle, the wise court magician we have come to know and love is cast in the now familiar role of Arthur's councilor and consultant to the Knights of the Round Table. Here we find the familiar stories of the sword in the stone, and Merlin's final demise at the hands of the Lady of the Lake, or Morgan le Fey, or Morgause, or Vivian, or any number of other dark witches, depending on whose account we read.

His story is still being written, but what has finally emerged is a picture of a hinge figure—the last of one tradition and the harbinger of another:

- He closes out the age of the Druids as Arthur and his knights begin to embody the triumph of mystical British Christianity.

- He is a sylvan man of wild forests that drip with mystery and magic, but he engineers the construction of Camelot, the archetypal city built on a hill.

- He represents an age of dark magic that gives way to a culture of shining light and virtuous chivalry.

- He rebuilds Stonehenge, the "Giant's Dance," but dedicates it as a symbol of light in the darkness.

- He sleeps in a crystal cave, but like Arthur, the "once and future king," will re-awaken when he is again needed. (Perhaps that time is now!)

All this is to say that if we spend a lot of time trying to identify a historical figure named Merlin, we are apt to miss the big picture. What is important is the total story, not an individual man who might once have existed in Wales, or maybe Cornwall, or perhaps Scotland, or wherever else scholars have tried to find him.

Was Nennius an imposter? Is Geoffrey of Monmouth a credible historian? Did the *Vulgate Cycle*'s confusing, overlapping, and changing stories get it right? Is there any historical relevance to the mystical Merlin who still dominates the so-called "New Age?"

Who cares? Those are each interesting literary studies, to be sure, and assure the job security of many an Arthurian scholar. But we are interested in what the stories *mean*. How do they apply to life in the 21st century? How do they relate to our times? How do they help us understand ourselves better? How do they help us live more fulfilling lives? That's what will consume us in the following pages. To study Merlin the Magician is to study a mystery for the ages, and unlock the metaphysical magic that permeates every one of us.

We know it's there. It peeks out of its 21st century shroud from time to time, and reveals its presence in déjà vu, dreams, out-of-body and near-death experiences, and daytime visions. It also is revealed from time to time in telescopes, microscopes, and the mathematics of theoretical physicists.

In short, Merlin is alive and well. He is as relevant as today's newspaper headlines. His story is our story, the story of the 21st century.

THE TEXT

From *The History of the Kings of Britain*: Geoffrey of Monmouth
Translated by J.A. Giles in 1848
Book VI: Chapter XVII

King Vortigern had recourse to magicians, who advised him to build a very strong tower for his own safety, since he had lost all his other fortified places. Accordingly, he came to Mount Erir, where he assembled workmen and ordered them to build the tower.

The builders began to lay the foundation, but whatever they did one day, the earth swallowed up the next, so as to leave no appearance of their work.

Vortigern, being informed of this, consulted with his magicians, who told him that he must find a youth who never had a father, kill him, and then sprinkle the stones and cement with his blood, for by those means, they said, he would obtain a firm foundation.

Messengers were dispatched away over all the provinces, to inquire about such a man. In their travels they came to a city, called afterwards Kaermerdin, where they saw some young men playing before the gate. Being weary with their journey, they sat down to see if they could meet with what they were in quest of.

Towards evening, there happened a quarrel between two of the young men, whose names were Merlin and Dabutius. In the dispute, Dabutius said to Merlin: "You fool, do you presume to quarrel with me? I am descended of royal race. As for you, you never had a father."

At that, the messengers looked earnestly upon Merlin and asked the by-standers who he was. They told him that it was not known who was his father, but that his mother was daughter to the king of Dimetia, and that she lived in St. Peter's church among the nuns of that city.

Chapter 1: Merlin and the Legend

> *King Vortigern had recourse to magicians,*
> *who advised him to build a very strong*
> *tower for his own safety, since he had lost*
> *all his other fortified places.*
> *Accordingly, he came to Mount Erir,*
> *where he assembled workmen*
> *and ordered them to build the tower.*
> *The builders began to lay the foundation,*
> *but whatever they did one day,*
> *the earth swallowed up the next,*
> *so as to leave no appearance of their work.*

The story of Merlin is set within the timeframe of a troubled, fractured land. Julius Cesar had landed in *Britannia*, or the "Land of the Britons," on August 26, 55 BCE, fresh from his conquest of Gaul. His mission was to conquer the native Celts.

That being said, however, the Romans didn't really conquer the land for another hundred years. And even when they did, they never were able to make much progress in

Wales, Cornwall, and the country north of Hadrian's Wall, including all of Scotland. It took time, but finally they established enough of a military presence in southern Britain to bring some semblance of peace and security for the people. Roman order and discipline exerted a significant influence from the time of Vespasian and Claudius for more than four centuries, until 410 of the Common Era.

The Roman church likes to claim they "Christianized" the British people, beginning with the mission of Augustine in 597 CE, but in actuality, there were Christian missions established as early as the first century. As a matter of fact, although the belief has been discredited by most mainstream historians, there are those who claim Christianity was brought to Britain by none other than Joseph of Arimathea, described in all four biblical Gospels as a righteous and wealthy man, who volunteered his own tomb as a burial place for Jesus after the crucifixion. Although he was a member of the Jewish Sanhedrin, he believed Jesus to be the promised Messiah, and along with Nicodemus, another member of the Jewish ruling council, he made sure there was a proper burial. He also was said to have somehow obtained the cup that was used at the last supper, known throughout history as the Holy Grail. Some believe that it was this cup which was used to catch the blood that flowed from Jesus's side when he was stabbed by what has come to be known as the Spear of Destiny.

Later authors claimed Joseph of Arimathea amassed his fortune in the tin trade. In order to do that, he must have made journeys to Cornwall, land of tin mines, and the major source of that precious product used throughout the bronze age. If so, he certainly would have become familiar with British traders. Some legends link him to Jesus, claiming that he was Mary's uncle, and that the boy Jesus might even have journeyed to Cornwall with him. Thus it is that William Blake would later write his famous poem, *Jerusalem*, sometimes referred to as England's second national anthem:

"And did those feet in ancient time
Walk upon England's mountains green:
And was the Holy Lamb of God,
On England's pleasant pastures seen?"

Legend goes on to claim that St. Philip, one of the original twelve disciples of Jesus, sent Joseph, along with the Holy Grail, to England, following the resurrection. There Joseph built Britain's first church. Some call it the first Christian church ever built anywhere in the world. He hid the grail in the well at Glastonbury. To this day, it's called the Chalice Well. Glastonbury, surrounded by shallow water in those days, is a long-time candidate for the location of the Isle of Avalon, where Arthur and Guinevere are said to have been buried. Early monks claimed to have discovered their grave remains, but most scholars think such claims were a publicity stunt to increase tourism dollars.

Early Christianity in Britain was quite different from the Roman brand that arrived with St. Augustine. It tended to leave a lot more room for so-called "pagan" beliefs. It embraced more of what later was declared heretical. In other words, it wasn't nearly so dismissive of magicians such as Merlin. Even centuries later, during the time that just preceded Merlin, there was intensive theological disagreement between Britain and Rome. Pelagius, who lived at the same time as Augustine of Hippo, and later became a favored source of inspiration for the Protestant reformers of the 16th century, was a British theologian who favored free will and asceticism.

Augustine, who believed in predestination, original sin, and the impossibility of humans earning any measure of their salvation by good works alone, declared Pelagius a heretic. When Pelagianism was ruled a heresy by Rome, many British believers simply ignored the decree.

With all this going on, the common folk tended to embrace all of the above. They went to Mass on Sunday, celebrated Saint's days throughout the year, prayed to St. Mary and Joseph, and put out offerings for the local gods every evening at dusk.

Somehow the whole culture was held together by the Roman presence in southern England, and it managed to hang on until 410 CE. That's when so-called "barbarians" began to nip away at Rome's eastern European borders, making such inroads that the emperor was forced to pull his troops out of Britain and bring them back to protect the homeland.

Almost overnight, Britain was thrown into chaos. The wealthy class, who considered themselves to be Roman citizens, were left with a lot of money, and no protection. Many buried their precious jewels and golden table ware, and then departed for safer lands, hoping to someday return and reclaim their wealth. Perhaps their clandestine endeavors were quietly observed by the Celts who remained behind. Ever since that time there have been stories about finding a pot of gold at the end of the rainbow.

Such unprotected wealth attracted other folks, as well. Angles and Saxons from western Europe began to dream of easy pickings across the channel, and launched exploratory raids. British kings from Cornwall, Wales, and northern provinces, as well as those who now commanded those areas formerly guarded by Romans troops in the south, began to rise up against one another, each hoping to be the central figure that could dominate all of Britain, and be the one king who could rule them all.

Such were the aspirations of Vortigern, styled *Superbus Tyrannus*, or "King of Britain," by the scholar later to become known as the Venerable Bede. Lacking the troops needed to enforce his will, Vortigern made a fatal error. He hired Saxon mercenaries under Hengist and Horsa to fight for him against the Picts and Scots, and paid them with land grants. He had sowed the wind. Now he was about to reap the whirlwind. Gildas, the 6th century historian, later blamed Vortigern for the loss of Britain.

At this point, it's important to remember our central premise when it comes to reading the Merlin stories. Did all this happen as we have just summarized it? Is this an account of real history?

Well, maybe. But maybe not. Modern archeologists tend to downplay a good deal of the former theories concerning a 5th century Saxon invasion, as opposed to a relatively peaceful migration. It's very possible that Vortigern never really existed at all, let alone at this particular time. But that's not important to our study. Whether or not these events occurred, this is the setting that gave birth to the tales of Merlin. It is within this context that his story is presented.

With this in mind, we can begin to establish a theme from which to assign meaning to the characters of the Merlin saga.

Interpreting the story in this manner:

Vortigern represents a person who is trying to bring order out of chaos for the wrong reasons. In the midst of a fragmented and vulnerable culture, he seeks personal power and prestige.

He is the personification of ego run amuck.

As his life crumbled around him, Vortigern still professed belief in a magic that could restore sanity and order. He thus had a troupe of magicians by his side. But he doubted their power, and had no personal spirituality that he could draw from that was sufficient to help him through the crisis. He possessed no moral compass; no ethical anchor to secure him amidst the storms of life. Having "*lost all his other fortified places*," or philosophical ideals necessary to stand upon a firm foundation of morality in a chaotic world, he sought to build "*a strong tower*" that could protect him in perilous times. But he was building that tower on false premises, and it would not stand.

We all are familiar with people like that. They have abandoned any central structure of ethics or morality in their life which will guide them through confusing times. When they entertain positions of power, such as that of professional politicians and national leaders, they often spend more time *keeping* their job than *doing* their job.

Sometimes we all, to varying degrees, experience such times. Our lives seem to be fragmented and falling apart. Our belief structures crumble around us. We seek a fortified position, a solid framework of faith to which we can anchor ourselves. We feel lost and adrift in confusing times. When that happens, if we have failed to developed a basic, spiritual reference point which will serve as a moral guide, we will certainly fall.

During the 1970s, the whole world witnessed such a slow-motion collapse. Richard Nixon, then president of the United States, was faced with a fragmented country eerily similar to the situation Vortigern faced. The moral structure that dominated America in the 40s and 50s, which would later prove to be as riddled with hypocrisy as the power of ancient Rome, weakened in popular culture, leaving chaos in its wake. With rioting in the streets, an unpopular war that was later proved to be fought on false premises, a government in disarray, and cultural norms being turned inside out, with "old white guys" holding the reins and "flower-power hippies" asserting their rights alongside armed militants urging revolution, and oppressed people staging riots in the street, it was a dark, dangerous, fragmented time in American history.

Richard Nixon, having abandoned his peace-oriented Quaker roots, found himself bereft of philosophical underpinning. He summoned his court magicians, who had names such as Ehrlichman, Dean, Haldeman, Segretti, and Magruder, who in turn enlisted others such as E. Howard Hunt and G. Gordon Liddy. They suggested that Nixon fortify himself in a strong castle of deceit and illegal activities now called the Watergate Scandal.

In this way of reading the story:

Court magicians symbolize those insiders who follow traditional, institutional, hierarchical systems of government or religion, but have long since ceased to believe in them, other than using them as a means to an ego-centered end.

Instead of following the Quaker principles taught him since birth, Nixon followed the advice of his "court magicians," and, in effect, hired the Saxons. We'll define the meaning of "Saxons" in a moment, but in the end, it destroyed him. His "strong tower" collapsed around him, leaving him adrift on the seas of history.

In every time of chaos, we need strong, inner, moral principles to follow, no matter what the consequences may be. In the midst of hate, we need to practice love. In the midst of despair, we need to depend upon hope. In a time of war, we need to search for peace. When the name of the game is power, we need to practice gentleness.

It may seem impossible. We may try to justify evil actions on the basis of what seems like necessity. But in the end, those actions will fail. Deceptive and cowardly means are never justified by a supposed necessary end. They will lead to a downhill spiritual slide that can take us to the very brink of Hell.

That's what happened to Vortigern:

Vortigern, being informed of this,
consulted with his magicians,
who told him that he must find a youth
who never had a father, kill him,
and then sprinkle the stones and cement with his blood,
for by those means, they said,
he would obtain a firm foundation.

It was a ridiculous solution. Vortigern was to mimic the early Christian story by cruelly sacrificing the product of a virgin birth, as did King Herod of old. Who could believe such a thing?

Possibly his advisors knew the solution was ill advised. After all, how many children have you ever met who never had a human father? Maybe they just hoped that the impossibility of the whole thing would prevent anything from happening at all, and that the idea would just fade away.

Alas, it was not to be.

Messengers were dispatched away over all the provinces,
to inquire about such a man.
In their travels they came to a city,
called afterwards Kaermerdin,
where they saw some young men playing before the gate.
Being weary with their journey,
they sat down to see if they could meet
with what they were in quest of.
Towards evening, there happened a quarrel between two
of the young men,
whose names were Merlin and Dabutius.
In the dispute, Dabutius said to Merlin:
"You fool, do you presume to quarrel with me?
I am descended of royal race.
As for you, you never had a father."

At that, the messengers looked earnestly upon Merlin and asked the by-standers who he was. They told him that it was not known who was his father, but that his mother was daughter to the king of Dimetia, and that she lived in St. Peter's church among the nuns of that city.

The text now introduces us to Merlin for the first time. He is about to step on to the stage of history. But remembering the metaphorical meaning we assigned to Vortigern and his court magicians, we can first focus in on the Saxon threat that led to Vortigern's downfall. According to this reading of the text:

Saxons represent the intruding values of a materialistic culture that threaten the ethical and moral principles which underlie the very essence of what it means to be a spiritual human being.

If a mature, grounded, person thinks about a given situation dispassionately, free from the temptations of ego, he or she usually knows, or at least has a pretty good idea, what is right and what is wrong. Unfortunately, we are seldom free from the temptations of ego.

Consider a few examples:

- Politicians enter their career believing in the values of patriotism and, in the words of Abraham Lincoln, government of, by, and for the people. They are elected to serve a particular constituency. But when opposition arises that threatens the implementation of those beliefs, the temptation to bring about that which they hold dear by employing questionable tactics rears its ugly head. "Just this once," they say. "It's for the greater good." And they channel their inner Vortigern by making sweetheart deals with questionable donors or making false claims about their opponents. "After all," they equivocate, "my motives are pure."

- A man in a position of power uses his position to satisfy a passing sexual lust with a willing underling. "I deserve it," he says. "I'm under a lot of tension. I'm important, so I'm allowed." Forgetting the moral anchor of his underlying marriage vows and public trust, he somehow justifies his actions and then lies about the affair when it becomes public. Ask anyone from Bill Clinton and Tiger Woods to Donald Trump and Jim Baker about this one.

- A woman who faces unarguable prejudice in the

fields of business or entertainment compromises herself in order to get the promotion or role she undoubtedly deserves. "The system is rigged against me," she decides. And she's right. It is. So she does things she knows are demeaning at best, and immoral at worst.

- An author, musician, or artist creates work that he or she is told will sell and make money, rather than exploring those subjects that are important and close to their heart. The world of the arts is thus commandeered by materialistic gatekeepers who seek only profit.

- Religious leaders, who for many years lusted after a larger public pulpit than the one afforded them on Sunday mornings, make deals with political figures who promise them the world if they will only sell their souls. To their chagrin, the same men who wield political power engage in practices far removed from the morals of traditional religion, leaving the religious leaders with the ethical impossibility of defending what they used to call "sin."

The problem with each of these situations, and all of us are familiar with similar scenarios, is that when our initial decision is one of compromise, it paves the way down a slippery slope that leads to ruin.

Herein we find the eternal relevance of Merlin' story.

"The country is fragmented," said Vortigern. "I would make a good leader. Why not make a deal with the devil" who, in this metaphor, is represented by Saxon hoards? The problem is that the price of the compromise was land. The Saxons didn't just help him achieve his goals. They slowly moved in and settled down. He soon found himself in an untenable situation, and in taking the advice of his court-sanctioned magician "experts," he compounded his error and compromised the principles that might have saved him from ultimate destruction.

This offers us a clue about the metaphorical implications found in Vortigern's "strong tower."

The "strong tower" represents a moral, ethical place of security, in which we hope to shelter ourselves from the changing, swirling, shifting sands of cultural ambiguity.

Once we compromise our spiritual principles, we

give the enemy, in this case the temptation to say that the means justify the end, a toehold. It becomes easier and easier to do it some more. The lies get bigger. The compromises more severe. Eventually we find ourselves oppressed by the very forces we employed to fight the original suppression. The cure is worse than the disease. Soon, we don't control the temptations. They control us. And we, like Vortigern of old, find ourselves searching for "*a strong tower*" in which we can defend ourselves.

But by then it's too late. The tower, built as it is on shifting sands of ethical and moral indecision rather than the strong moral foundation which we have long since abandoned, keeps collapsing under its own weight. We become so distraught we are open to any suggestion, even one as inherently evil as sacrificing an innocent child. Deep down inside, we know it won't work. But we are so desperate and lost, we will try anything.

Surprisingly, however, the solution offers hope. Merlin, who represents the long abandoned metaphysical magic we have rejected in our quest for materialistic, egotistical success, does produce a miracle. Just not the one we hoped to bring about through our meager efforts.

Before we turn to Merlin, let's recap:

- Vortigern represents a person who is trying to bring order out of chaos for the wrong reasons. In the midst of a fragmented and vulnerable culture, he seeks personal power and prestige. He is the personification of ego run amuck.

- Court magicians symbolize those insiders who follow traditional, institutional, hierarchical systems of government or religion, but have long since ceased to believe in them, other than using them as a means to an ego-centered end.

- Saxons represent the intruding values of a materialistic culture that threaten the ethical and moral principles which underlie the very essence of what it means to be a spiritual human being.

- The "strong tower" represents a moral, ethical place of security, in which we hope to shelter ourselves from the changing, swirling, shifting sands of cultural ambiguity.

The stage is now set for the introduction of Merlin the Magician. If he didn't really exist, someone would have had to invent him. He was the missing link that paved the way for the triumph of King Arthur. He also represents the missing link that we need to rediscover if today's fragmented society is ever to be restored to wholeness.

He's not hard to find. He sleeps within each one of us, awaiting only our summons to awake from the darkness within.

THE TEXT

From *The History of the Kings of Britain*: Geoffrey of Monmouth
Translated by J.A. Giles in 1848
Book VI: Chapter XIX

Merlin was brought before King Vortigern. Attentive to all that had passed, he approached the king and said to him, "For what reason am I and my mother introduced into your presence?"

"My magicians," answered Vortigern, "advised me to seek out a man that had no father, with whose blood my building is to be sprinkled, in order to make it stand."

"Order your magicians," said Merlin, "to come before me, and I will convict them of a lie."

The king was surprised at his words and presently ordered the magicians to come and sit down before Merlin, who spoke to them after this manner:

"Because you are ignorant what it is that hinders the foundation of the tower, you have recommended the shedding of my blood for cement to it, as if that would

presently make it stand. But tell me now, what is there under the foundation? For something there is that will not suffer it to stand."

The magicians began to be afraid and made him no answer.

Then said Merlin, who was also called Ambrose, "I entreat your majesty to command your workmen to dig into the ground. There you will find a pond which causes the foundations to sink."

This accordingly was done and presently they found a pond deep underground, which had made the wall to give way.

After this Merlin went again to the magicians and said, "Tell me ye false sycophants, what is there under the pond."

But they were silent.

Then said he to the king, "Command the pond to be drained, and at the bottom you will see two hollow stones, and in them two dragons asleep."

The king made no scruple of believing him, since he had found true what he said of the pond, and therefore ordered it to be drained. When that was done, he found as Merlin had said, and now was possessed with the greatest admiration of him. Nor were the rest that were present less amazed at his wisdom, thinking it to be no less than divine inspiration.

Chapter 2: Merlin and Earth Magic

Merlin was brought before King Vortigern. Attentive to all that had passed, he approached the king and said to him,
"For what reason am I and my mother introduced into your presence?"
"My magicians," answered Vortigern,
"advised me to seek out a man that had no father, with whose blood my building is to be sprinkled, in order to make it stand."
"Order your magicians," said Merlin,
"to come before me, and I will convict them of a lie."

When the world was first introduced to Merlin through the magic of literature, he was not so much an enchanter as he was a prophet. In Welsh poetry his name was *Myrddin*, and he had no connection to Arthur at all. Instead, he was a wild man of the forest and even, truth be told, sometimes described as a madman. It took Geoffrey of Monmouth, some 650 years after Merlin's story was first told, to turn him into the more familiar *Merlin Ambrosius* (in Welsh, *Myrddin Emrys*), by connecting him with *Ambrosius Aurelianus*, brother to Uther, and perhaps even father to Merlin.

Welsh audiences adopted the new character, though, and he soon took on the mantle that the whole world came to know and love. Merlin soon attracted an aura of mystery and enchantment. He became a prophet who could see the future, and mentor to the young Arthur. He was a magician who could work miracles and produce wonders. If a king had Merlin at his side, it was said, he could accomplish anything.

The image of Merlin that the world eventually embraced was that of a hinge figure. He bridged the gap between pagan Celts and Christian Romans. Last of the Druids, first of the new order, he became a powerful symbol that left an indelible mark on history. To this very day, there are those who believe he still haunts the dark places of Celtic legend. Buried but not forgotten, you can't help but bump into him when you walk the dark, dripping, forest paths of the nighttime British landscape.

When we first meet him, he fills a role that is famously celebrated throughout mythology. With no earthly father, he is a product of Father Sky and Mother

Earth. He thus personifies a union of the spiritual and material creation. Although the most well-known current example of this typology is Jesus Christ, Greek mythology is full of characters who emerged from the marriage of earth and sky. The sky was called "Father" and the Earth "Mother." Uranus was the Father God who fell in love with Gaia, the Earth Mother. They had many children together. In this way, humans, being both spirit and flesh, contained the mythological DNA of both parents. Father Sun ruled the day. Mother Earth, symbolized by the moon, ruled the night. Heaven and Earth, Night and Day, Light and Dark—all was one, and in harmony; two sides of the same coin.

The Japanese told a similar story when they claimed that Izanami, the female goddess, gave birth to Amaterasu, the sun, and Tsuki-yumi, the moon. It's a mythological theme found all around the world. In the well-known tale of the Garden of Eden, Adam had no earthly mother. The Persian Mithras was born of a virgin, as was, in some stories, the Hindu Buddha and Iranian Zoroaster. Egyptian mythology tells the same tale about Horus.

Virgin births are so common throughout the world that, in some cases, a religious founder wasn't really taken seriously unless his mother had no earthly husband.

Such is the case with Merlin. Just as he is a hinge between two different cultural and spiritual traditions, he represents a melding of spirit and flesh, religion and science, and, in our day, we might add quantum theory and Newtonian physics. When he appears, things happen. Time and space are altered. Nothing is quite as it appears.

We can picture it best by walking alone in the dark woods at night. Nothing is there after dark that isn't there in bright daylight. But it doesn't feel that way. Noises are louder, moon shadows cast strange shapes, and things are much more mysterious.

Merlin represents the edge; the place where two worlds meet. That's where the magic occurs. Even modern science teaches us that life is, at root, an illusion. What seems solid and real is not, in fact, the way the way things are. Merlin stands at the epicenter of reality and illusion. He is a metaphorical Higgs Field, wherein energy takes on mass.

A wonderful cultural adaptation of the paradox that juxtaposes reality with illusion was captured in an episode of the television series *Northern Exposure*. The series is set in the mythical town of Cicely, Alaska. A traveling carnival finds itself stranded for a few days, awaiting the repair of its bus. The owner of the traveling circus is a physicist-turned-magician, who quickly finds a kindred soul in the self-taught mystic who is also the town's radio announcer.

The announcer capitalizes on the performer's presence to attempt to get his own personal handle on some of the truths that underlie existence. He decides to ask the carnival physics-guy-turned-magician why he changed jobs. What he learns is that, "On the subatomic level, everything is so bizarre, so unfathomable. With magic you have some control."

This prompts the announcer to later reflect to his audience:

"When we think of a magician, the image that comes to mind is Merlin. Long white beard, cone-shaped hat, right? You know. Well, in one version of this Arthurian legend, the archetypal sorcerer retires. Checks out of the conjuring biz. His reason? The rationalists are taking over. The time for magic is coming to an end. Well, ol' Merlin should have stuck around because those same rationalists trying to put a rope around reality suddenly found themselves in the psychedelic land of physics. A land of quarks, gluons, and neutrinos. A place that refuses to play by Newtonian rules. A place that refuses to play by any rules. A place better suited for the Merlins of the world."

Eventually the two have a follow-up conversation that runs something like this:

ANNOUNCER: "This has been bugging me for a long time. I was doing some reading on the super string thing atomic theory. I was having a hard time ... because my math is weak ... but it seems to me that when you get into the onion of an atom and you get to the smaller and smaller particles, you find that you really don't have any particles at all."

CARNI: "Yeah."

ANNOUNCER: "So subatomic particles might just really be vibrating waves of energy?"

CARNI: "Correct. Right. Listen. No mass, no-thing."

ANNOUNCER: "The essential building block of everything is nothing?"

CARNI: "All is an illusion. That's what I hated about the [physics] business. What are you supposed to do with information like that?"

The announcer again muses to his radio audience about what he discovered from the conversation:

"If there is nothing of substance in the world; if the ground we walk on is just a mirage; if reality itself really isn't real—what are we left with? What do we hang our hat on? Magic! The stuff not ruled by rational law."

With this as a background, we can now identify the mythological symbolism surrounding Merlin the Magician:

Merlin represents the conjunction of matter and spirit, reality and illusion, magic and everyday life. He takes us beyond our normal existence, and reveals our dreams. He reminds us that there is more to life than normal experience, and offers hope to those forced to live in an increasingly sterile world.

Keeping this description firmly in mind, we can now continue with Merlin's story:

The king was surprised at his words and presently ordered the magicians to come and sit down before Merlin,

> *who spoke to them after this manner:*
> *"Because you are ignorant what it is that hinders*
> *the foundation of the tower,*
> *you have recommended the shedding of my blood*
> *for cement to it,*
> *as if that would presently make it stand."*

Earlier we discovered that Vortigern's "strong tower" represents a moral, ethical place of security in which we hope to shelter ourselves from the changing, swirling, shifting sands of cultural ambiguity. With the Saxon threat at our very doorstep, such a place should keep us safe from compromising our principles and giving in to weak positions of accommodation. A leader, whether he or she is a political, religious, business, or social presence of authority, needs such a spiritual place of strength—something to believe in. The temptations to stray from moral authority can be too great to resist sometimes.

But if that tower is going to stand it needs to be built on a bedrock of ethical and spiritual foundational principles. Anything less will cave in, as we see so often when political or religious leaders fall from grace after having abandoned their initial moral beliefs. With that as a context, Merlin now asks a question for the ages:

"But tell me now, what is there under the foundation? For something there is that will not suffer it to stand."

Beginning in the late 1980s, the Catholic Church experienced a sea change of public opinion, as the past indiscretions and sexual sins of hundreds of priests began to come to light. The scandal soon cascaded in an ever-increasing downhill slide, and now continues well into the 21st century.

Protestant Evangelical leaders were quick to back Donald Trump for president because of his identification with much of their social agenda. But when the future president was caught on film demeaning women, they found themselves in a difficult position. Rather than withdraw their endorsement, they were forced to justify Trump's obvious failings as a moral "man of God."

Historically, political leaders were often protected from similar exposure by reporters who tacitly agreed to overlook such activities in print. Eisenhower and Kennedy benefited from the custom. But beginning with the impeachment of Bill Clinton, because of an affair conducted in the Oval Office, the practice could no longer be sustained.

With the advent of the #MeToo movement, which went viral in October of 2017, similar activities now quickly become fodder for public consumption. Powerful men in the fields of entertainment, business, politics, and religion could no longer get away with sexual intimidation while expecting an "old boy's network" to hide their sins. Their "strong tower" was proved false because it was built on a weak foundation of lies and cover-ups. When it fell, it came down with a crash. The "court magicians" who had utilized building materials such as bribes, threatened slanders, hush money, public humiliation, extortion, and the promise of career rewards, had built a tower that could not stand up to the gaze of public scrutiny. When the Band-Aid was torn off the festering wound, many famous men found they had trusted a network of allies that could no longer protect them.

How the mighty have fallen. And the process continues. Merlin's evocative question echoes right down to our present day: "*Tell me now, what is there under the foundation? For something there is that will not suffer it to stand."*

Is it any wonder that "*The magicians began to be afraid and made him no answer*"?

Today the swirling milieu of failing ethics, morality, and spiritual discernment is in need of the voice of Merlin. We need his advice now as never before.

He still stands ever ready to speak truth to a world which more and more seems to be following the advice of court magicians who manipulate traditional bastions of spirituality. Remember, Merlin is alive and well and lives within each of us. To hear his message, we need only listen to the still, small voice that speaks within the human heart. That's from where the message will come. It won't echo forth from Washington DC, London, Rome, Moscow, Beijing, or any national capitol. It won't be heard in the form of a scientific edict or academic treatise. The next, needed, leap forward in human evolution will take place in the human heart. Merlin will awake and come forth from the crystal cave in which he has been imprisoned since before the age of industrialization.

What will the message be? What will it consist of?

Merlin lore suggests it will not be a call to something new, but rather to something old. It will not be a new teaching that we need to learn. It will be found in an old message that we have forgotten. He will advise us to return to the wisdom and strength of Mother Earth. He will caution us to rediscover the metaphorical dragon of primal Earth Energy.

Then said Merlin, who was also called Ambrose,
"I entreat your majesty to command your workmen
to dig into the ground.
There you will find a pond
which causes the foundations to sink."
This accordingly was done and presently they found a
pond deep underground,
which had made the wall to give way.
After this Merlin went again to the magicians and said,
"Tell me ye false sycophants,
what is there under the pond."
But they were silent. Then said he to the king,
"Command the pond to be drained,
and at the bottom you will see two hollow stones,
and in them two dragons asleep."
The king made no scruple of believing him,

since he had found true what he said of the pond, and therefore ordered it to be drained.

If Vortigern's tower was ever going to stand, it had to be anchored solidly in the earth. Only the strength emanating from that which gave us birth in the first place will do.

It may *seem* as though from the first indication of simple matter to the solid formation of rock and hill, from the fires of Mother Earth's warm heart to the cold of her polar ice, from the smallest, one-celled amoeba to the greatest of her stolid land creatures, that the continuing theme of nature is, on the surface at least, survival of the fittest. It may *appear* that only the strong and best adapted survive to reproduce, and that nature "red in tooth and claw" dominates our environment. That, after all, is the law that constitutes the insistent whine of modern court magicians.

But what about so-called abstract concepts such as beauty and love—the things that make life worth living? Where did they come from? Can we find them in the survival of the fittest? Do they exist in untimely death? Indeed, in death at all? In the long evolutionary march of creation, can they survive betrayal and war, inhumanity and brutality?

Creatures of time and space will probably answer with a resounding "NO!" Those who believe that Alpha and Omega, "Beginning and End," anchor two ends of a straight arrow of time, cannot conceive of such a thing. But the Merlin of legend doesn't think of time and space in those terms. He knows that Alpha and Omega inhabit identical, overlapping points on a great circle. He believes that the beginning and the end are one and the same, and sees not the past and future but only the ever-present Now. Gaia herself knows. Consciousness sings the song. Energy writes the music. But sublime concepts such as compassion, beauty, and love are the theme. A "strong tower" built on anything less cannot stand.

So it is that even as Gaia endures the crucifixion of pavement and strip mall, even as the nails of industrial mining pierce her flesh and a crown of thorny development is pressed upon her bowed head, even as rivers of her polluted blood empty into life-giving waters, from the very brink of death her call goes forth in love, "Forgive them! They know not what they do."

We are in trouble, says Merlin, because the false "strong tower" of modern technology, the tower that was supposed to be our shelter in the storm, our position of strength which would offer sanctuary in a turbulent world, the place where we thought we could hide from the metaphorical, Saxon-like enemies of hypocrisy, greed, lust for power, and materialism, which we invited into our presence to aid us achieve a false security, was built on a swamp.

Moral principles did not guide the growth of late 20th century technology. It was fueled by greed. Ethical premises did not undergird western industrialism. At its base lay the lust for economic dominance. Political influence is, and probably always was, motivated by the desire for personal power, not social justice.

Greed, economic dominance, and the lust for power compromise the very building blocks suggested by modern court magicians to those who, like Vortigern, seek to build a "strong tower" in which they can hide from the trials and tribulations of the world. They hope that if they can somehow accumulate enough money, influence, possessions, insurance, and power, they will be protected from the storms of life. Having fought their way to the top, they decide to circle their proverbial wagons so as to remain aloof from the trials of ordinary people. They conspire to pass laws that will protect their hard-won assets. They try to influence politicians who will build a wall between them and society. In some cases, their contributions are even viewed as insurance against divine intervention. It is not by accident that the verbiage of many modern insurance policies contains payments made for damages derived from flood, fire, and other "acts of God."

These are the methods of, not all, but certainly many, of the Vortigerns among us. They are aided and abetted by their advisors—their "court magicians"—who argue for more of the same. "Build your strong tower of industrial, technological, economic, and material wealth," they argue. "It will protect you from the gathering storm of Saxon hoards which you utilized to propel you to the top in the first place."

But such a tower, says Merlin, is built on porous ground. Its foundations are not anchored solidly to the basic principles of existence bestowed upon us by Mother Earth, who conceived us and gave us life. Human-inspired technology cannot save us if it harms our environment. If industrial waste, which pollutes the planet, is greater than the comfort it is meant to provide, the whole industry will fall of its own weight. If we split the atom, the building block of material life, to obtain a limitless source of energy, but do not demonstrate the ethical and spiritual maturity to harness that power in productive ways, we will certainly destroy ourselves.

Merlin cautions us to return to a deep appreciation of that which nurtured us for uncounted millennia before we took such a terrible turn in our history. Ages ago we began to think of the earth as a simple resource, rather than a sacred, nurturing, ground of being. Like metaphorical Saxons of old, we pillaged the earth rather than respected and revered it. We cut down its forests, paved over its meadows, burned its fossil fuels without any thought, and dammed up its water supplies. We built where we should never have built, and destroyed that which should have lasted forever. We sought to build our tower of refuge on a swamp of conflicted needs, and now are being reminded, in harsh consequences that grow ever more insistent, of our tragic error.

And what do we feel will hold it all together? The voice of those who counsel more of the same call out for the blood of Merlin. They want to dispel any ideas of magic. They tell us to sacrifice any hope of aid other than that which got us into this trouble in the first place. Technology will save us only if we slake its foundations with the blood of antiquated superstition.

The voice of Merlin, contradicting the false wisdom of modern court magicians, needs to once again be heard echoing throughout our world. Only then will those who might listen really hear. It's there within each one of us. We all know it speaks the truth. It's only those in power who refuse to listen.

But maybe, just maybe, another miracle will transpire. Perhaps the Vortigerns of the world will finally wake up. Only then will the prophetic text come to pass:

When that was done, [Vortigern] found as Merlin had said, and now was possessed
with the greatest admiration of him.
Nor were the rest that were present
less amazed at his wisdom,
thinking it to be no less than divine inspiration.

With that being said, let's recall for a moment, before we continue, what the text teaches us about the presence of Earth Magic:

- **Merlin represents the conjunction of matter and spirit, reality and illusion, magic and everyday life.**

- **He takes us beyond our normal existence, and reveals our dreams.**

- **He reminds us that there is more to life than normal experience, and offers hope to those forced to live in an increasingly sterile world.**

Those words were true in the day the Merlin story was first told. As we shall soon see, they are equally true today.

THE TEXT

From *The History of the Kings of Britain*: Geoffrey of Monmouth
Translated by J.A. Giles in 1848
Book VI: Chapter XIX

As Vortigern, king of the Britons, was sitting upon the bank of the drained pond, the two dragons, one of which was white, the other red, came forth, and, approaching one another, began a terrible fight. They cast forth fire with their breath. But the white dragon had the advantage and made the other fly to the end of the lake. And he, for grief at his flight, renewed the assault upon his pursuer, and forced him to retire.

After this battle of the dragons, the king commanded Ambrose Merlin to tell him what it portended.

Merlin, bursting into tears, delivered what his prophetical spirit suggested to him, as follows:

"Woe to the red dragon, for his banishment hastens on. His lurking holes shall be seized by the white dragon, which signifies the Saxons whom you invited over. The red

denotes the British nation, which shall be oppressed by the white. Therefore, shall its mountains be leveled as the valleys, and the rivers of the valleys shall run with blood. The exercise of religion shall be destroyed and churches be laid open to ruin. At last, the oppressed shall prevail and oppose the cruelty of foreigners.

Chapter 3: Merlin and the Dragon

Something there is that doesn't love a wall, that wants it down."

These words, famously penned by the American poet Robert Frost in his 1914 poem, *Mending Wall*, artistically describes Vortigern's problem. The walls of his "strong tower" refused to stand. Something kept causing them to fall. Merlin pointed out the fact that he was building on what amounted to a swamp, but that there was more beneath the surface. Indeed, when it comes to understanding what appears to be simple physical reasons for why things happen the way they do, there are often underlying spiritual principles at work.

Doctors, for instance, are quick to point out that mental stress can cause physical illness. "Freudian Slips" reveal feelings we didn't know we had. People who fear death often die the deaths they most fear. Over and over again, if we keep our minds alert and our thoughts open to discern underlying meanings, we can recognize that there is usually more to reality than meets the eye.

In this case, Geoffrey of Monmouth is quick to point out that Vortigern's wall fell not simply because it was built on a weak foundation. There were underlying spiritual principles at work as well.

> *As Vortigern, king of the Britons,*
> *was sitting upon the bank of the drained pond,*
> *the two dragons, one of which was white,*
> *the other red, came forth,*
> *and, approaching one another, began a terrible fight.*
> *They cast forth fire with their breath.*
> *But the white dragon had the advantage*
> *and made the other fly to the end of the lake.*
> *And he, for grief at his flight,*
> *renewed the assault upon his pursuer,*
> *and forced him to retire.*

At the bottom of it all lay the dragons.

Dragon symbolism is different in Eastern traditions than in western mythological lore.

In the East, the dragon symbolizes vitality and strength. It is understood to be the raw energy of nature, the ultimate energy of the earth itself. The serpent that experiences growth and renewal when it sheds its skin is in a continual process of regeneration and growth. It is worshipped as the guardian of secret places, and is immortalized in seasonal parades, where it symbolizes new beginnings.

In the time when the Arthurian legends were written, the western concept of the dragon dominated the Christian church. There, the dragon represented evil. Anyone who has read JRR Tolkien's *Lord of the Rings* is familiar with this interpretation. The dragon is a terrifying force of nature, that consumes all in its path as it gathers gold and treasure. It doesn't use the treasure. It just hoards it. The only way to access the wealth is to slay the guardian.

The evil dragon symbol is found in western mythology and monotheistic religious texts. It is there in the form of a serpent in the Garden of Eden, and is identified as "that old serpent, the Devil" just before the final battle of Armageddon. In North and Central American mythology, it appears in the guise of a rattle snake. It is a creature meant to be conquered and destroyed, destined to fall before the materialistic and technological power of a humanity that is separate from, and superior to, the powers of nature.

But in early Merlin tales, the dragon is also a creature of the old, earth-centered, Pagan belief system that derived its strength from the power of Mother Earth. It is found in "dragon lines" that carry vital earth *chi*, or life energies, as they "snake" their way through nature. The intersections of these energy lines were often marked by great megalithic structures that some people believe were constructed to magnify and amplify this vital earth force. In other words, they were built on holy ground.

It appears as though most of these megalithic monuments had an astrological connection that pointed to something in the heavens. The general rule of thumb is summarized in the ancient doctrine, "As above, so below." Even the venerable, formulistic *Lord's Prayer* of the Christian Church contains the clause, "Thy will be done on earth as it is in heaven."

On the morning of a solstice, stand in the center of Stonehenge, visit Newgrange, climb a sacred mountain, or trek back into the Peruvian jungle to one of the great pyramids, and you will certainly understand that there is as much mathematical precision at any of those ancient places as you will find in the most complicated observatory built today. If you factor in degree of difficulty, there is even more. Many a contemporary astronomer, if challenged, could not duplicate our ancestor's work if they were forced to forego their sophisticated computers and telescopes and limit themselves to working only with observation and stone.

But the battling dragons of Merlin's prophecy carried much more than astrological significance. They told the future.

After this battle of the dragons,
the king commanded Ambrose Merlin to tell him
what it portended.
Merlin, bursting into tears,
delivered what his prophetical spirit
suggested to him, as follows:
"Woe to the red dragon,
for his banishment hastens on.
His lurking holes shall be seized by the white dragon,
which signifies the Saxons whom you invited over.
The red denotes the British nation,
which shall be oppressed by the white.
Therefore, shall its mountains be leveled as the valleys,
and the rivers of the valleys shall run with blood.

> *The exercise of religion shall be destroyed*
> *and churches be laid open to ruin.*
> *At last, the oppressed shall prevail*
> *and oppose the cruelty of foreigners.*

According to Merlin, the red dragon, which symbolized the British people, would be oppressed by the white dragon, which symbolized the Saxon armies. But in the end, the red dragon would win. Presumably this represented the triumph of Arthur, although history tells us the Saxons eventually did establish themselves and dominate Celtic Britain, at least until the Norman invasion.

By the time of the Arthurian sagas, Arthur had come to represent the Church Triumphant. His chivalrous, pure-of-heart, and dedicated Christian Knights of the Round Table went about the countryside searching for Holy Grails and other religious artifacts. But Merlin, last of the Druids and the mysterious magician of the old ways, was still secretly the power behind the throne.

History is written by the victors. In this case it was written by a Christian cleric who had a vested interest in putting to rest the old Dragon religions that pointed to the stars rather than Heaven, and derived its strength from

Mother Earth instead of the Sun or, more appropriately, the Son, Jesus the Christ. By the time Geoffrey wrote *The History of the Kings of Britain,* the time of the Dragon was over. But in Merlin's time the old legends still carried a lot of weight.

With that as background, what meaning do the red and white dragons have for us today?

Each color is significant. Red is the color of fire and blood. It is usually associated with determination, passion, desire, and love. Valentines are red. Red roses are associated with love. The red cross is the emblem of both a life-giving medical emergency organization and the Knights Templar, who were noted for their ferocity in war. Red is thus an intense, emotional color. Scientists tell us that even gazing upon it can raise our blood pressure a bit and increase respiration rates.

White, on the other hand, is associated with goodness and purity. The white "light at the end of the tunnel" is often remembered by those who undergo near-death experiences. Brides traditionally where white gowns to symbolize both virginity and a new beginning. The color white, when shown through a prism, is shown to contain all the colors of the rainbow. It is the color of perfection.

We can put all this together and conceptualize a duality that lies at the heart of every human endeavor. If the dragon is a symbol of earth energy, then:

The red and white dragons symbolize the presence of duality in the material world.

In the world in which we live, everything exists in pairs, and is experienced as the inverse of its opposite. There can be no up without a down, no fast without a slow, no long without a short. Cold and hot, old and new, black and white, winning and losing, make up the world of duality that we know and experience for our whole lives. We can't escape it, because we are a part of it.

In western religious traditions we are taught to identify with one pole and fight against the other. Monotheistic religions are built on the idea of resisting evil and seeking after the good. A red devil sits on one shoulder and whispers evil thoughts into one ear, while a white angel sits on the other and cautions us to do good. It is so much a part of our culture that we hardly even think about it anymore. There is truth and there is falsehood. Choose one. This is the unspoken but powerful force that dominates our philosophy. If a TV news commentator states a principle, we want to hear "the other side," assuming there are only two sides of every issue to be considered. For every god there is a devil. For every *Luke Skywalker* there is a *Darth Vader*. When we depart the side of goodness and truth we go over to the dark side.

Try to think of a movie or story in which good and evil are not somehow pitted against each other. You will be hard pressed to find even one. The eternal battle of duality is so central to our experience that we even make good guys and bad guys out of opposing sports teams.

Before Galahad could complete his quest, he had to overcome the evil Green Knight. Before Jesus could enter into his ministry, he had to journey into the wilderness to overcome Satan. Before the Buddha could become enlightened, he first had to overcome the three temptations of Mara, the devil.

The battle between good and evil is often thought to be at the center of every problem on earth. How did a good God create a world in which there is evil? How is the human race, which contains such wonderful, positive potential, capable of such unmitigated evil as world wars, nuclear devastation, torture, and climate destruction on a planetary scale? Why do even the best of us, with sharp, stinging words, so often "hurt the one we love, the one we shouldn't hurt at all," as the Mills Brothers used to remind us in song? Why do bad things happen to good people and, conversely, good things happen to bad people? Either God *cannot* prevent evil, in which case God is not all-powerful, or God *will not* prevent it, in which case God is not good. The name for this field of study is Theodicy.

But what if there is more than one "other side?" What if there are more than two sides to a coin? What if life is much more complicated than a simple binary choice?

If duality signifies pairs of opposites, then one half of every such pairs is probably uncomfortable. The natural human tendency, then, is to identify with that which is good, comfortable, or otherwise desirable.

Siddhartha Gautama, known to the world as the Buddha, was the first to recognize that this was impossible. In a flash of enlightenment, he came see that in a world consisting of duality, unless both poles of opposites are embraced, one cannot be content, because both poles are real and make up the fabric of life. To remain insulated from one pole or the other is to live in denial. Denying, or even ignoring, death and sickness, for instance, doesn't make them less real. All it creates is anxiety, because the human psyche knows they are inevitable.

The Buddha's profound insight is now recognized in every culture on Earth. It is so common that we forget Siddhartha was the first to put it into words, and to frame it in a way that easily transcends culture and language. His idea was profound in its simplicity. He taught that the secret of happiness is to find the middle way between the poles so we can enter into a transcendent sphere that encompasses both.

Applying this insight forces us to completely change the way we think about the Saxon "invasion" of Britain, and Merlin's place in the epic. Both the two warring dragons contained within them qualities of good and evil. They had to, because they both represented human cultures that came with all the frailties and faults, as well as potential and possibility, common to all people everywhere. If we choose one side and call it good, the other automatically becomes evil.

Historians such as Geoffrey of Monmouth were tempted to do just that. He identified with Britain, so the Saxons were bad. It was as simple as that. But if you were a Saxon, just trying to find a new life on land you had legitimately been given in payment for services rendered, you undoubtedly had a different point of view.

Things are no different today. In August of 1945, many Americans justified dropping atomic weapons of mass destruction on civilian populations of Japanese, because they thought of themselves as good guys trying to end a war. They tried not to think about the fact that thousands of those who died horrible deaths were just regular people trying to go about their daily lives and get by in terrible times, victims of politicians and government officials who had their own agendas. In order to sleep at night, Americans needed to come to at least the unconscious conclusion that every one of those Japanese civilians was an evil person who willingly, and with full, responsible capabilities, supported an evil empire who had bombed Pearl Harbor. Without that mindset they would be forced to admit that The United States of America was the only nation in the entire history of the world that deployed and actually used atomic weapons. That's a tough burden to shoulder. Far better to consider all Japanese of that time as "them"—an evil enemy.

Consider the arguments that are usually called forth to justify any act of atrocity.

- "They did it first, so my actions are justified."
- "We may have done some bad things, but we've done so much good that we need to overlook them."
- "So-and-so is a lying politician, but he is accomplishing some things I agree with."

On and on it goes. We will go to almost any lengths to justify immoral behavior.

All this is to say that we need to look beneath the surface when it comes to the warring dragons of Geoffrey's story. It's easy to jump on his bandwagon and say the British were good and the Saxons were bad. But history itself reveals that, given time, folks often manage to get along. They didn't always make war. Sometimes they made love. Modern DNA evidence points to the fact that Celtic-

Anglo-Saxon bloodlines make up the oldest surviving original families in today's British Isles.

Given this reality, the red and white warring dragons reveal something very important to every contemporary analysis of this ancient story. Our attempts to build a strong tower of ethical, moral, and spiritual principles will fail if they are built on false premises and shaky foundations, but even the best of human intentions reveal an underlying weakness. No matter how good and honorable our intentions, we need to be constantly monitoring our motives. The dragons of duality underlie all our feeble intents and purposes. The best of us can slip and fall. The worst among us are capable of great things. Beware the one who claims perfection. Even the heroes of old, if they were to suddenly appear among us, would probably be seen to have feet of clay.

That's why Merlin is best seen as a legend. If an actual Merlin once lived, and we could talk to him today, he would undoubtedly disappoint.

Maybe this insight is more important than it at first seems. We all have a tendency to judge ourselves severely. We like to think of ourselves as good people, and most of us are. But we are capable of bad things as well. And for those who have a low self-image, don't be so hard on yourself. You have untapped reservoirs of goodness within you. None of us are as bad or as good as we think we are. That's called being human.

As is often the case when it comes to deep, penetrating, psychological insight, Eastern sages were way ahead of western philosophers on this subject. At least 2,500 years ago the symbol of the *Tao,* or *Dao,* captured the essence of duality.

Notice in this well-known symbol that light and dark exist intertwined in a circle of duality. But within the light there is a small dark spot, and within the dark there is a small light spot. Each pole thus contains its opposite. In the same way, there is some good in every evil, and a bit of evil hidden away in every good.

Picture a beautiful spring scene in your mind. The sky is a deep blue, with a few white, puffy clouds hanging quietly beneath a brilliant sun. The grass has turned a bright green, and robins hop joyfully upon its surface.

Trees are starting to leaf out, and the promise of summer lies over all.

It's a beautiful picture, isn't it? But concentrate on those robins for a minute. What are they doing on your imaginary lawn? They're eating worms! Good food for a robin. Worms are keeping it alive and feeding its young ones. But what about the worm? Your beautiful red-breasted ambassador of spring could equally be a feathered monster from on high. It all depends on your perspective.

That's what the Dao is all about. It puts things in perspective. Life on earth in the material realm consists of tension. Your good fortune could be somebody else's misfortune. The shirt that keeps you warm might have been made in a Chinese sweatshop. The rain that waters your garden might have caused a flood for someone else. The sun that shines on your picnic might be shriveling a farmer's cash crop at the same time. Good and bad. Bad and good. Good within bad. Bad within good. That's what constitutes the school of life.

Those who wrote about Merlin understood this. They didn't couch their wisdom in the form of a philosophical treatise. Instead, they told a story. An essay or technical paper is soon forgotten. But a story is forever.

Thus it is that the story of Merlin the Magician has stood the test of time, and still speaks to us today. It reminds us to look at the big picture of life whenever we are overwhelmed by the details. When Merlin confronted the dragons, he was penetrating to the very depths of what it means to be human while living in a world of duality.

To recap this very simple but profound truth:

- **The red and white dragons symbolize the presence of duality in the material world.**

Having faced that truth head on, and recognizing the deeply stressful and depressing implications of how it was to play out in human affairs, he "*burst into tears*." Nevertheless, he was now ready to put it to practical use in the material world.

Legends and myths don't always end with a "happy ever after." As long as good and evil exist, one will never completely triumph over the other. But recognizing the existence of both at least prepares us to live a productive life. In Merlin's case, even in the midst of his despair at what was to come, he decided to build a monument that stands to this very day. It was time to dance.

THE TEXT

From *The History of the Kings of Britain*: Geoffrey of Monmouth
Translated by J.A. Giles in 1848
Book VII: Chapter XIX - XII

Following the defeat of his enemies, Aurelius the king summoned the consuls and princes of the kingdom together at York, where he gave orders for the restoration of the churches which the Saxons had destroyed. He himself undertook the rebuilding of the metropolitan church of that city, as also the other cathedral churches in that province.

Even London had not escaped the fury of the Saxons, and he beheld with great sorrow the destruction made in it, and began restoration. Here he settled the affairs of the whole kingdom, revived the laws, and restored the right heirs to the possessions of their ancestors. In these important concerns was his time wholly employed.

From hence he went to Winchester to repair the ruins of it. When the work was finished there, he went, at the instance of bishop Eldad, to the monastery near Kaercaradoc, now Salisbury, where the consuls and princes, whom the wicked Saxon, Hengist, had treacherously murdered, lay buried.

At this place was a convent that maintained three hundred friars, situated on the mountain of Ambrius, who had been the founder of it. The sight of the place where the dead lay made the king, who was of a compassionate temper, shed tears and at last enter upon thoughts as to what kind of monument to erect upon it. He thought something ought to be done to perpetuate the memory of that piece of ground, which was honored with the bodies of so many noble patriots who died for their country.

For this purpose, he summoned together several carpenters and masons, and commanded them to employ the utmost of their art, in contriving some new structure to serve as a lasting monument to those great men. But they, in diffidence of their own skill, refused to undertake it.

Tremounus, archbishop of the City of Legions, went to the king and said, "If anyone living is able to execute your commands, Merlin, the prophet of Vortigern, is the man. In my opinion, there is not in all your kingdom a person of a brighter genius, either in predicting future events or in mechanical contrivances. Order him to come to you and exercise his skill in the work which you design."

Aurelius, after he had asked a great many questions concerning Merlin, dispatched several messengers into the country to find him. After passing through several provinces, they found him in the country of Gewisseans, at the fountain of Galabes, which he frequently resorted to. As soon as they had delivered their message to him, they conducted him to the king, who received him with joy, and, being curious to hear some of his wonderful speeches, commanded him to prophesy.

Merlin made answer: "Mysteries of this kind are not to be revealed unless there is great necessity. If I should pretend to utter them for ostentation or diversion, the spirit that instructs me would be silent and would leave me when I should have occasion for it."

Therefore, the king would not urge him any longer about his predictions, but spoke to him concerning the monument which he designed.

"If you are desirous," said Merlin, "to honor the burying-place of these men with an ever-lasting monument, send for the Giant's Dance, which is in Killaraus, a mountain in Ireland. For there is a structure of stones there which none of this age could raise without a profound knowledge of the mechanical arts. They are stones of a vast magnitude and wonderful quality, and if they can be placed here, as they are there, round this spot of ground, they will stand forever."

At these words Aurelius burst into laughter. "How is it possible to remove such vast stones from so distant a country, as if Britain was not furnished with stones fit for the work?"

Merlin replied, "I entreat your majesty to forbear vain laughter, for what I say is without vanity. They are mystical stones, and of a medicinal virtue. The giants of old brought them from the farthest coast of Africa and placed them in Ireland. There is not a stone there which has not some healing virtue."

When the Britons heard this, they resolved to send for the stones. To accomplish this business, they made choice of Uther Pendragon, who was to be attended with fifteen thousand men. They also chose Merlin himself, by whose direction the whole affair was to be managed. A fleet *being therefore got ready, they set sail, and with a fair wind arrived in Ireland.*

Upon his arrival he placed in order the engines that were necessary, took down the stones with an incredible facility, and gave directions for carrying them to the ships. This done, they with joy set sail again, to return to Britain; where they arrived with a fair gale, and repaired to the burying-place with the stones.

Chapter 4: Merlin and the Giant's Dance

Following the defeat of his enemies,
Aurelius the king summoned the consuls and princes of the
kingdom together at York, where he gave orders for the
restoration of the churches
which the Saxons had destroyed.
He himself undertook the rebuilding
of the metropolitan church of that city,
as also the other cathedral churches in that province.
Even London had not escaped the fury of the Saxons,
and he beheld with great sorrow
the destruction made in it, and began restoration.
Here he settled the affairs of the whole kingdom,
revived the laws,
and restored the right heirs
to the possessions of their ancestors.
In these important concerns
was his time wholly employed.
From hence he went to Winchester
to repair the ruins of it.
When the work was finished there, he went,

*at the instance of bishop Eldad,
to the monastery near Kaercaradoc, now Salisbury,
where the consuls and princes, whom the wicked Saxon,
Hengist, had treacherously murdered, lay buried.*

Spirituality never occurs in a vacuum. We often think that gurus continuously walk around engaged in great thoughts and noble inclinations, but even the Dalai Lama has to eat breakfast and, I imagine, take out the trash once in a while. Jack Kornfield wrote a wonderful book about enlightenment called, *After the Ecstasy, The Laundry*. That about sums it up.

In this chapter we're going to read about how Merlin the Magician built Stonehenge, or, as it was often called, the Giant's Dance. The whole story is very entertaining and imaginative, but without any historical merit. Stonehenge was built over the course of thousands of years and was already incredibly old by the time the Merlin legend was first written down. As for it being a dance of giants, who were somehow transformed into stone, perhaps Sue Kendrick sums it up best in a piece she wrote for TimeTravel-Britain.com:

They call this place the Giants' Dance, and say a wizard built it with stones he stole from Erin. By his arts, he flew them through the air and set them down on the great plains of Salisbury, and made a ring of power to endure forever. The wizard was no conjuror of cheap party tricks, but Merlin, Arch-Druid of all Albion and the Giants Dance—Stonehenge—built, according to Geoffrey of Monmouth, to commemorate the treacherous slaying of Vortigern at nearby Amesbury by Hengist the Saxon. A likely tale? Of course not, but it is just this kind of mystique that has given this broken ring of stones its hypnotic appeal and turned it into a major World Heritage site.

The story begins as Aurelius the king is busy with some housekeeping chores. He is rebuilding the kingdom after its near destruction by Saxon invaders. It is immediately obvious that Geoffrey of Monmouth is engaged in public relations as much as anything. Aurelius "*himself undertook the rebuilding of the metropolitan church of [London], as also the other cathedral churches in that province.*" That probably consoled the Christian religious establishment of his day.

But he mended some political fences as well: "*Here he settled the affairs of the whole kingdom, revived the laws, and restored the right heirs to the possessions of their ancestors. In these important concerns was his time wholly employed.*"

Geoffrey is about to delve into some deep magical work on Salisbury plain, but first he takes pains to point out that the magic takes place in the midst of daily activities. The business of the country was moving along, and it is only in the context of day-to-day activity that spiritual wonders take place.

This insight reminds us of a simple but profound truth. Most of us live a humdrum, daily chores-type existence. So it is important to remember:

Magic is the exception, not the rule.
It is always around us and ready to work its wonders,
but we have to be alert to it

or we'll miss it when it takes place.

This truth is illustrated by what happens next.

*At this place was a convent
that maintained three hundred friars,
situated on the mountain of Ambrius,
who had been the founder of it.
The sight of the place where the dead lay made the king,
who was of a compassionate temper,
shed tears and at last enter upon thoughts
as to what kind of monument to erect upon it.
He thought something ought to be done
to perpetuate the memory of that piece of ground,
which was honored with the bodies of so many noble
patriots who died for their country.
For this purpose,
he summoned together several carpenters and masons,
and commanded them to employ the utmost of their art,
in contriving some new structure
to serve as a lasting monument to those great men.
But they, in diffidence of their own skill,
refused to undertake it.
Tremounus, archbishop of the City of Legions,*

> went to the king and said,
> "If anyone living is able to execute your commands,
> Merlin, the prophet of Vortigern, is the man.
> In my opinion, there is not in all your kingdom
> a person of a brighter genius,
> either in predicting future events
> or in mechanical contrivances.
> Order him to come to you and exercise his skill
> in the work which you design."

The old texts often contain the most wisdom, and sometimes our familiarity with them makes us overlook passages which can profitably teach us. In this case, two words pretty much sum up what is going on at this point in the story, and they remind us of the importance of honest evaluation and humility.

Here they are: "Know thyself."

Aeschylus, the ancient Greek playwright, used them in his play *Prometheus Bound*. Both Socrates and Plato employed them with great effect in their teachings. They were inscribed over the entrance to the temple at Delphi.

Ralph Waldo Emerson immortalized the phrase in his poem *Gnothi Seauton* ("Know thyself"): "Then take this fact into thy soul: God dwells in thee."

The first trick is to accept what Emerson stated so simply. The second is to act on it.

When Aurelius sought to build a great monument, he "*summoned together several carpenters and masons,*" presumably the best in the land. He instructed them to "*employ the utmost of their art, in contriving some new structure to serve as a lasting monument.*"

This was no doubt a builder's dream job. If the court artisans fulfilled expectations, their careers and reputations would be set for life. But following the old maxim, "Know thyself," they deferred to one more qualified than themselves. Probably with some reluctance, they directed the king to Merlin.

As Clint Eastwood's character "Dirty Harry" once said, "A man's got to know his limitations." It is a good thing to know when you're ready to take on a task, and when you're not.

Ludwig van Beethoven died six years before Johannes Brahms was born, but Brahms, master of many classical styles and genres, put off writing his first symphony for twenty years. Symphonies were Beethoven's forte. He had mastered the idiom and produced nine of the greatest ever written.

Quite frankly, Brahms felt he was not ready. When asked why he was hesitating, he once said, "You can't have any idea what it's like always to hear such a giant walking behind you."

He eventually got to the point where he finally felt he was ready, and eventually triumphed with his majestic first symphony, which is sometimes referred to, by those in the know, as *Beethoven's Tenth.*

Brahms understood the truth of the old saying. He knew himself, and didn't proceed until he felt he was ready.

There is a fine line of distinction between honest evaluation and courage to attempt the unknown. If we always waited until we thought we were ready to take on a task, we'd probably be paralyzed with fear and never begin in the first place. But until the time is right, we need to be careful.

Once again, we can turn to the ancient Greek philosophers for help. When they talked about chronological, every-day-type time they used the word χρόνος ("chronos"). It's the word that forms the basis of our concept of chronological, or sequential, time. But when they talked about real "strike while the iron is hot," "now is the time," "let's do this" time, they used the word καιρός ("kairos"). That refers to the supreme moment, the instant things come together, and you have to move now or forever hold your peace.

The builders sensed that this was such a time. According to the story, at least, they were about to undertake a project that was bigger than time—bigger than all of them. They knew skill wasn't enough. It was time for magic.

Aurelius, after he had asked a great many questions
concerning Merlin, dispatched several messengers
into the country to find him.
After passing through several provinces,
they found him in the country of Gewisseans,
at the fountain of Galabes,
which he frequently resorted to.
As soon as they had delivered their message to him,
they conducted him to the king,

who received him with joy, and, being curious to hear some of his wonderful speeches, commanded him to prophesy. Merlin made answer: "Mysteries of this kind are not to be revealed unless there is great necessity. If I should pretend to utter them for ostentation or diversion, the spirit that instructs me would be silent and would leave me when I should have occasion for it."

Therefore, the king would not urge him any longer about his predictions, but spoke to him concerning the monument which he designed.

"If you are desirous," said Merlin, "to honor the burying-place of these men with an everlasting monument, send for the Giant's Dance, which is in Killaraus, a mountain in Ireland. For there is a structure of stones there which none of this age could raise without a profound knowledge of the mechanical arts. They are stones of a vast magnitude and wonderful quality, and if they can be placed here, as they are there, round this spot of ground, they will stand forever."

At these words Aurelius burst into laughter.

"How is it possible to remove such vast stones

from so distant a country,

as if Britain was not furnished with stones

fit for the work?"

Merlin replied,

"I entreat your majesty to forbear vain laughter,

for what I say is without vanity.

They are mystical stones, and of a medicinal virtue.

The giants of old brought them

from the farthest coast of Africa

and placed them in Ireland.

There is not a stone there

which has not some healing virtue."

When the Britons heard this,

they resolved to send for the stones.

To accomplish this business,

they made choice of Uther Pendragon,

who was to be attended with fifteen thousand men.

They also chose Merlin himself, by whose direction the

whole affair was to be managed.

A fleet being therefore got ready, they set sail,

and with a fair wind arrived in Ireland.

Upon his arrival he placed in order the engines that were necessary, took down the stones with an incredible facility, and gave directions for carrying them to the ships. This done, they with joy set sail again, to return to Britain; where they arrived with a fair gale, and repaired to the burying-place with the stones.

Even Merlin, however, didn't rush in where angels fear to tread. He was familiar with magic enough to know that we cannot enter into its potent sphere without due consideration: "*Mysteries of this kind are not to be revealed unless there is great necessity. If I should pretend to utter them for ostentation or diversion, the spirit that instructs me would be silent and would leave me when I should have occasion for it.*"

There is a time for craft and skill. Those are qualities much respected in *Chronos* time. But this was a *Kairos* moment, and everyone of import, except for the king, apparently, recognized it.

Using contemporary language, every *Star Wars* fan knows that there comes a moment when you have to turn off the computer and trust the force if you're going to destroy the evil death star. It *Kairos* time. To put it bluntly:

There comes a time when craft and skill are not sufficient. Only magic will do.

Aurelius, being a typical non-believer, thought he knew better. He "*burst into laughter*," a typical response. Those who think they are running the show, back then as today, usually don't trust the efficacy of magic to get things done in the real world. They may offer "thoughts and prayers," and pay lip service to spiritual help from "the man upstairs," or other such patronizing euphemisms, but when push comes to shove, they consider material techniques far more practical than spiritual principles, such as faith.

Anyone who ever watched the popular, and important, TV series M*A*S*H soon came to see that William Christopher's character, Father Mulcahy, was a mere figurehead in the OR. The real power was wielded by the doctors. The good priest functioned well when he was soothing fears or practicing psychology. But when it came time to operate, he was pushed aside. Skill always trumps faith.

When Merlin revealed how the magic would work, he, too, was ridiculed. He insisted the stones to be used in building the monument that would stand for all time were to be found only in Ireland. This offended Aurelius' civic pride. "*How is it possible to remove such vast stones from so distant a country, as if Britain was not furnished with stones fit for the work?*"

But Merlin stood fast, even in the midst of bureaucratic pessimism. "*I entreat your majesty to forbear vain laughter, for what I say is without vanity.*"

There comes a time when every magician needs to stand fast and hold to the truth, even in the midst of worldly pessimism and ridicule. Indeed, that's the test of true magic. How much are you willing to believe? How firm is your faith? When the time comes, will you have the courage shown by Luke Skywalker, when he turned off his targeting computer and trusted the force? If you ask for proof, will you believe your prayer is answered when serendipity occurs?

This was a test for Merlin, just as much as it was for Aurelius and his worldly staff of politicians. If he backed down, assuming for the moment that we accept the historicity of the story, we never would have heard from him again.

But Merlin didn't back down. He went on to rebuild the Giant's Dance. And only then do we realize that in order for big things to happen, we have to pave the way with small acts of confidence-building that eventually lead to faith.

Without Stonehenge there could be no Arthur. Without the Giant's Dance there could be no new age.

Merlin understood the great lesson upon which the future swayed:

- **Magic is the exception, not the rule. It is always around us and ready to work its wonders, but we have to be alert to it or we'll miss it when it takes place.**

- **There comes a time when craft and skill are not sufficient. Only magic will do.**

What we have here is a classic conflict of egos. Ego involves identity. It asks the question, "Who am I, and with what am I identified?"

A "worldly" ego, for lack of a better term, identifies itself within the individual as separate from everybody else. It chooses its friends on the basis of their ability to provide something ego desires. It will choose pleasure over pain, gain over loss, comfort over discomfort, and immediate satisfaction over long-term health. It identifies totally with the material world and recognizes that with the death of its host, its time is over. It will do everything possible to sustain life, even a miserable life of sickness and pain, over death, which signifies its end. There is no ego in the Source—no "I" in heaven. There is only unity.

Aurelius represents earthly ego in this story. Even as he contemplated death, which, after all, was the whole reason he wanted the Giant's Dance rebuilt, he could think only of what he could gain out of it.

Merlin, on the other hand, although also in possession of a healthy dose of ego, as are we all, identified not with worldly skills, crafts, and explanations, but with a greater world of earth magic. Yes, he was a creature of ego.

That's what happens to all of us when we are born into this life. But having an ego does not mean we have to employ it in the service of selfishness. Instead, while fully recognizing our own needs and wants, we can choose, in this world of duality, to identify with that which is good and wholesome. In this case, Merlin chose to identify with the power of earth magic instead of worldly political power.

And so, the fleet was launched. Against all odds, the stones were brought home to Britain, **erected by magic** and, according to legend, music.

That being accomplished, the world was now ready to receive the once and future king.

THE TEXT

From *The History of the Kings of Britain*: Geoffrey of Monmouth
Translated by J.A. Giles in 1848
Book VII: Chapter XIX - XII

After the death of Aurelius, Uther become king. After many battles, when he had established peace in the northern provinces, he went to London. The Easter following, he ordered all the nobility of the kingdom to meet at that city in order to celebrate the great festival. The summons was everywhere obeyed, and there was a great concourse from all cities to celebrate the day. So the king observed the festival with great solemnity, as he had designed, and very joyfully entertained his nobility, of whom there was a very great muster, with their wives and daughters, suitably to the magnificence of the banquet prepared for them.

Having been received with joy by the king they expressed the same in their deportment before him. Among the rest was present Gorlois, duke of Cornwall, with his wife Igerna, the greatest beauty in all Britain. No sooner had the king cast his eyes upon her among the rest of the ladies than he fell passionately in love with her, and little regarding the rest, made her the subject of all his thoughts. She was the only lady that he continually served with fresh dishes, and to whom he sent golden cups by his confidants. On her he bestowed all his smiles and to her he addressed all his discourse.

Her husband, discovering this, fell into a great rage, and retired from the court without taking leave. Uther, therefore, in great wrath, commanded him to return back to court to make him satisfaction for this affront. But Gorlois refused to obey.

The king was highly incensed, and swore he would destroy his country if he did not speedily compound for his offence. Accordingly, without delay, while their anger was hot against each other, the king got together a great army, and marched into Cornwall.

Gorlois durst not engage with him, on account of the inferiority of his numbers, and thought it a wiser course to fortify his towns. As he was under more concern for his wife than himself, he put her into the town of Tintagel, upon the sea-shore, which he looked upon as a place of great safety. But he himself entered the castle of Dimilioc, to *prevent their being both at once involved in the same danger, if any should happen.*

The king, informed of this, went to the town where Gorlois was, which he besieged, and shut up all the avenues to it. Retaining in mind his love to Igerna, he said to one of his confidants, named Ulfin de Ricaradoch: "My passion for Igerna is such that I can neither have ease of mind, nor health of body till I obtain her. If you cannot assist me with your advice how to accomplish my desire, the inward torments I endure will kill me."

"Who can advise you in this matter," said Ulfin, "when no force will enable us to have access to her in the town of Tintagel? For it is situated upon the sea and on every side surrounded by it. There is but one entrance into it, and that through a straight rock, which three men shall be able to defend against the whole power of the kingdom. Notwithstanding, if the prophet Merlin would in earnest set about this attempt, I am of opinion that you might, with his advice, obtain your wishes."

The king readily accepted what he was so well inclined to believe, and ordered Merlin, who was also come to the siege, to be called.

Merlin, therefore, being introduced into the king's presence, was commanded to give his advice as to how the king might accomplish his desire with respect to Igerna, and he, finding the great anguish of the king, was moved by such excessive love.

He then said, "To accomplish your desire, you must make use of such arts as have not been heard of in your time. I know how, by the force of my medicines, to give you the exact likeness of Gorlois, so that in all respects you shall seem to be no other than himself. If you will therefore obey my prescriptions, I will metamorphose you into the true semblance of Gorlois, and Ulfin into Jordan of Tintagel, his familiar friend. I myself, being transformed into another shape, will make the third in the adventure. In this disguise you may go safely to the town where Igerna is, and have admittance to her."

The king complied with the proposal and acted with great caution in this affair. When he had committed the care of the siege to his intimate friends, he underwent the medical applications of Merlin, by whom he was transformed into the likeness of Gorlois, as was Ulfin also into Jordan, and Merlin himself into Bricel, so that nobody could see any remains now of their former likeness.

They then set forward on their way to Tintagel, where they arrived in the evening twilight and forthwith signified to the porter that the consul was come. The gates were opened, and the men let in, for what room could there be for suspicion when Gorlois himself seemed to be there present?

The king therefore stayed that night with Igerna, and had the full enjoyment of her, for she was deceived with the false disguise which he had put on, and the artful and amorous discourses wherewith he entertained her. He told her he had left his own place besieged, purely to provide for the safety of her dear self, and the town she was in. Believing all that he said, she refused him nothing which he desired. The same night therefore, she conceived of the most renowned Arthur, whose heroic and wonderful actions have justly rendered his name famous to posterity.

In the meantime, as soon as the king's absence was discovered at the siege, his army unadvisedly made an assault upon the walls and provoked the besieged count to a battle. Acting as inconsiderately as they, he sallied forth with his men, thinking with such a small handful to oppose a powerful army. But it happened that he was killed in the very first brunt of the fight, and had all his men routed.

After this bold attempt came messengers to Igerna, with the news both of the duke's death and of the event of the siege. But when they saw the king in the likeness of the consul, sitting close by her, they were struck with shame and astonishment at his safe arrival there, whom they had left dead at the siege. They were wholly ignorant of the miracles which Merlin had wrought with his medicines.

The king therefore smiled at the news, and embracing the countess, said to her: "Your own eyes may convince you that I am not dead, but alive. But notwithstanding, the destruction of the town and the slaughter of my men is what very much grieves me, so that there is reason to fear the king's coming upon us and taking us in this place. To prevent which, I will go out to meet him and make my peace with him, for fear of a worse disaster."

Accordingly, as soon as he was out of the town, he went to his army, and having put off the disguise of Gorlois, was now Uther Pendragon again. When he had a full relation made to him how matters had succeeded, he was sorry for the death of Gorlois, but rejoiced that Igerna was now at liberty to marry again. Then he returned to the town of Tintangel, which he took, and in it, what he impatiently wished for, Igerna herself. After this they continued to live together with much affection for each other, and had a son, whose name was Arthur.

Chapter 5: Merlin and the Child

After the death of Aurelius, Uther become king. After many battles, when he had established peace in the northern provinces, he went to London. The Easter following, he ordered all the nobility of the kingdom to meet at that city in order to celebrate the great festival. The summons was everywhere obeyed, and there was a great concourse from all cities to celebrate the day.
So the king observed the festival with great solemnity,
as he had designed,
and very joyfully entertained his nobility,
of whom there was a very great muster,
with their wives and daughters, suitably to the magnificence of the banquet prepared for them.
Having been received with joy by the king, they expressed the same in their deportment before him.
Among the rest was present Gorlois,
duke of Cornwall, with his wife Igerna,
the greatest beauty in all Britain.
No sooner had the king cast his eyes upon her among the rest of the ladies than he fell passionately in love with her, and little regarding the rest,

made her the subject of all his thoughts.
She was the only lady
that he continually served with fresh dishes,
and to whom he sent golden cups by his confidants.
On her he bestowed all his smiles.
and to her he addressed all his discourse.
Her husband, discovering this, fell into a great rage,
and retired from the court without taking leave.
Uther, therefore, in great wrath,
commanded him to return back to court to make him
satisfaction for this affront.
But Gorlois refused to obey.

What is it about sex that causes even the mightiest men to fall?

A long time ago, while studying the biblical tale of David and Bathsheba in preparation for an extensive seminar on the formation of Israel, I entered into a search to determine why a great king would risk his entire kingdom, all because of a moment of lust. This study coincided with the congressional proceedings currently being held to impeach president Bill Clinton on the basis of lying to cover up an alleged sexual encounter in the oval office.

I read Jung and Freud, historical biographies about world leaders, reports about the Kennedy brothers, and even salacious stories I had never heard about Albert Einstein, who had told his first wife not to expect fidelity in their marriage. This was before their divorce and his subsequent marriage to his cousin. He may have won a Nobel Prize in physics, but he was certainly not a candidate for any kind of sainthood.

I even learned some troubling things about who Gandhi slept with. The Mahatma himself, for heaven's sake!

Much to my surprise, I never satisfactorily concluded my search. Even today, with massive computer search engines at my disposal, I still have no idea what there is about a moment of lust that is so strong it can bring down a kingdom.

Millions of articles have been written about that fact that sex is a powerful force in human lives. But they don't explain why. They sometimes reach conclusions about wanting to propagate the species, but that doesn't make any sense. Most people engaged in illicit affairs try desperately *not* to propagate the species. Indeed, the trouble often *begins* with propagation. How many people have determined the course of their whole lives because a moment of lust produced a child that brought about a marriage that probably otherwise would not have occurred, and maybe even *should not* have occurred?

I read a lot of articles and research papers about sex being connected with spirituality. The ancient Hindu *rishis* used to call death "the orgasm that lasts forever." They associated enlightenment with that moment of sexual satisfaction when time seems to stand still, nothing else exists, and people have even been known to say, "Oh God!" Talk about a religious experience! On the one hand, at that moment, it is one of the few times in life that ego ceases to exist. Or maybe it exists in its strongest form. The verdict among psychiatrists is still out.

The old timers were probably on to something about sex and spirituality being somehow related, because thousands of articles have been written about the connection. And there is no doubt that this is partially the point of the Arthurian legend. Just as the fact remains that without David's sin with Bathsheba there would have been no Solomon, without Uther's sin with Igerna, there would have been no Arthur. Both sordid tales end in the innocent death of the betrayed husband, but somehow that fact is lost in the accomplishments of the child, who was conceived in immoral lust and grew to epic spiritual greatness, before himself succumbing due to his own sexual affairs.

Perhaps that is, in and of itself, somehow the point.
The text continues with great detail.

The king was highly incensed,
and swore he would destroy his country if he did not
speedily compound for his offence.
Accordingly, without delay,
while their anger was hot against each other,
the king got together a great army,
and marched into Cornwall.
Gorlois durst not engage with him,
on account of the inferiority of his numbers,
and thought it a wiser course to fortify his towns.
As he was under more concern for his wife than himself,
he put her into the town of Tintagel, upon the sea-shore,
which he looked upon as a place of great safety.
But he himself entered the castle of Dimilioc,
to prevent their being both at once involved
in the same danger, if any should happen.

The king, informed of this,
went to the town where Gorlois was,
which he besieged, and shut up all the avenues to it.
Retaining in mind his love to Igerna,
he said to one of his confidants,
named Ulfin de Ricaradoch:
"My passion for Igerna is such that I can neither have
ease of mind, nor health of body till I obtain her.
If you cannot assist me with your advice
how to accomplish my desire,
the inward torments I endure will kill me."
"Who can advise you in this matter," said Ulfin, "when no
force will enable us
to have access to her in the town of Tintagel?
For it is situated upon the sea
and on every side surrounded by it.
There is but one entrance into it,
and that through a straight rock,
which three men shall be able to defend against
the whole power of the kingdom.
Notwithstanding, if the prophet Merlin
would in earnest set about this attempt,
I am of opinion that you might,
with his advice, obtain your wishes."

When all else fails, pray. It's an old, old joke, but it's still very true. If there is no way to physically accomplish your goals, and you've tried everything else, turn to God.

One of my fondest moments as a struggling seminarian back in the early 70s took place one dark night when I thought I had pretty much come to the end of my rope. Academically I was in over my head, and beginning to suspect it. But the biggest problem was money. One dreadful Friday night, when I added up our bills and discovered that we owed $298 by Monday—no ifs, ands, or buts—I looked over at my wife, who was calmly reading a magazine on the couch, and said, "We're in trouble. We'd better pray."

She looked back at me, the aspiring clergyman who was going to win over the world by teaching people to have faith, smiled a beatific smile, and said, "Has it come to that?"

We laughed about it for a long time.

This story has a postscript. We did pray about it, of course, and the very next day we got a check in the mail for $300. A church that had somewhat supported me in the past had some money left over in their missions budget and decided to send it to us.

Now, what church ever has money "left over" in its missions budget? But they did. So we paid our bills and wound up with $2 extra. Know what we did? We went out and bought a cheap bottle of wine to celebrate! Who says God doesn't have a sense of humor?

In the case of Uther, however, his advisors didn't tell him to pray. They sent for Merlin.

The king readily accepted
what he was so well inclined to believe,
and ordered Merlin, who was also come to the siege,
to be called.
Merlin, therefore,
being introduced into the king's presence,
was commanded to give his advice as to how the king
might accomplish his desire with respect to Igerna,
and he, finding the great anguish of the king,
was moved by such excessive love.
He then said, "To accomplish your desire,
you must make use of such arts
as have not been heard of in your time.

I know how, by the force of my medicines,
to give you the exact likeness of Gorlois,
so that in all respects
you shall seem to be no other than himself.
If you will therefore obey my prescriptions,
I will metamorphose you into the true semblance of
Gorlois, and Ulfin into Jordan of Tintagel,
his familiar friend.
I myself, being transformed into another shape,
will make the third in the adventure.
In this disguise you may go safely
to the town where Igerna is, and have admittance to her."
The king complied with the proposal
and acted with great caution in this affair.
When he had committed the care of the siege to his
intimate friends he underwent the medical applications of
Merlin, by whom he was transformed into the likeness of
Gorlois, as was Ulfin also into Jordan,
and Merlin himself into Bricel,
so that nobody could see any remains now
of their former likeness.
They then set forward on their way to Tintagel, where they
arrived in the evening twilight and forthwith signified to
the porter that the consul was come.

The gates were opened, and the men let in, for what room could there be for suspicion when Gorlois himself seemed to be there present? The king therefore stayed that night with Igerna, and had the full enjoyment of her, for she was deceived with the false disguise which he had put on and the artful and amorous discourses wherewith he entertained her. He told her he had left his own place besieged, purely to provide for the safety of her dear self, and the town she was in. Believing all that he said, she refused him nothing which he desired. The same night therefore, she conceived of the most renowned Arthur, whose heroic and wonderful actions have justly rendered his name famous to posterity.

With this text we enter into a convoluted description of how Merlin was able to use his magic to change Uther's appearance, along with a small entourage, into that of Gorlois and his aides, so that Uther could get into the fortress of Tintagel and sleep with Igerna. It all went according to plan. You can read the details for yourself, so there is no need to dwell on them. What's important is the inclusion of a few small items.

First of all, notice the motivations of the two men, Merlin and Uther. Uther was moved by lust. His desire was strictly toward fulfilling his "*desire with respect toward Igerna.*" Merlin, on the other hand, "*finding the great anguish of the king, was moved by ... excessive love.*"

Something magical was about to happen, and the state of the two men's egos were at complete odds with one another. One experienced lust. One experienced love. Was one "right" and the other "wrong?" That leads us to a second observation.

Living, as we do, in a world of duality, we are almost forced to decide between the two. Of course, most of us will probably decide for Merlin and against Uther. After all, Merlin's position is by far the most noble and pure.

But consider this. If it hadn't happened like this, at this particular time, Arthur never would have been conceived. If Uther had waited, he and Igerna still might have had a child together, but it would have been someone else. This was the *Kairos* moment. The time was at hand. If the young king who would grow up to save Britain was going to be born, it had to be in this way.

What does this teach us?

A spiritual force above and beyond duality is at work in the cosmos, and sometimes breaks through into human affairs. When it does, we call it magic. It isn't always pretty.

Most religions are involved with the process of choosing right over wrong. There is a God, and there is a devil. Who will you follow? Thus, most religions are involved with what we call ethics. There are good choices and bad choices. "He who is not for us is against us." Joshua said it in the Hebrew scriptures, and Jesus said it in the New Testament. It seems simple enough.

But is it?

When Prince Siddhartha Gautama was born, a local priest visited the family compound and prophesied that the youngster would grow up to be either an emperor or a Buddha, an Enlightened One. One or the other. No in-between. This is the essence of duality.

Quite naturally, the child's worldly father preferred the former to the latter, so he sequestered young Siddhartha within the walls of the palace, hoping to discourage any untoward spiritual development by supplying everything the young man desired in the way of material delights.

But young men are curious, so one day Siddhartha had his chariot driver take him out into the real world. The journey changed his life.

Soon after departing the palace grounds the young prince encountered an old man. He had seen elders before, but this was an aged man who had not benefitted from the cosmetics money can obtain. Siddhartha began to suspect that life exacts a toll, and he wondered about the path his own life would take. Fear began to cloud his still-inexperienced mind.

If that weren't enough, he soon encountered a man who was afflicted by a hideous disease. With a shock, he thus discovered that life contains an element of suffering.

Then he caught his first glimpse of a corpse, and the reality of death was seared into his consciousness.

Siddhartha later reflected on the lessons he had learned from his excursion thus far. As quoted in Robert S. Ellwood and Barbara A. McGraw's book *Many People, Many Faiths*:

"I also am subject to death and decay and am not free from the power of old age, sickness and death. Is it right that I should feel horror, repulsion and disgust when I see another in such plight? And when I reflected thus ... all the joy of life which there is in life died within me."

His heretofore-held illusions had evaporated. He now knew he needed to place his trust in something besides wealth and family position. Pleasure could not prevent age, illness, or death, and so could not be the pathway to happiness.

Without knowing it, he had taken the first step down the path that leads to spiritual growth. Still unaware that he was about to completely change course in life, he was perplexed to come upon a holy man, who seemed quite content. Something within Siddhartha suddenly shifted. He took a leap of faith. His mind at once understood what his heart had already come to appreciate.

From that moment on, the dancing girls back home didn't do it for him anymore. He decided he had to study the meaning of life by becoming a holy man. His father, in trying to keep him from seeking a spiritual path, had instead catapulted the young man toward a destiny that would change the world. Siddhartha determined to go off on a journey of exploration, even though he didn't know where that journey would lead. If you had asked him what he was searching for, and how he even knew there was something worth finding, he probably could not have answered. But he knew he had to look for it.

There was still the matter of convincing his father who, as expected, refused to let the boy leave. In lieu of what would later occur, it is instructive to observe the young man's method for obtaining what he wanted. Siddhartha simply waited, saying he would not move until he had his father's consent.

Dinnertime came and went. Siddhartha stood patiently in place. It got dark outside, time for the household to go to bed. His father, sure that by morning the boy would return to his senses, said goodnight and retired to his sleeping chamber. But morning's light found the boy still standing in the living room, ready to succeed or die.

Needless to say, the young prince eventually got his way. Saying goodbye to his family, Siddhartha and his faithful charioteer left the family compound, never to return. He began to search for a reality he could trust.

For six years he wandered and studied. He talked with Brahmins, Hindu holy men. He learned yoga disciplines and meditation. He practiced extreme asceticism, eventually trimming his diet down to one grain of rice a day, and then deciding that since he could exist on one grain, why not try slicing it in half to make it last twice as long? Eventually he became so thin and emaciated that it was later said of him that a person could grasp Siddhartha's backbone from the front.

Even after all this, enlightenment eluded him. He joined a group of traveling holy men, none of whom were making any more progress along the spiritual path than he was. They had nothing new to teach him.

Terribly discouraged, he resorted to the technique he had successfully used with his father. Seating himself beneath a type of fig tree known as a Bo tree (sometimes called a *Bodhi* tree, or "Tree of Knowledge"), he vowed he would meditate right there, not moving until he either reached enlightenment or died.

There in the wilderness of his own confusion he met Mara, the devil, who tempted Siddhartha with the traditional three temptations.

First, the temptation of the flesh. Three beautiful women walked by, begging him to follow. (Legend does not explain why three beautiful women were interested in an emaciated man whose backbone could be grasped from the front!)

Second, the temptation of the spirit. Ferocious demons attempted to frighten him enough to make him flee from his place beneath the Bo tree.

Smiling, Siddhartha simply touched the ground upon which he sat, saying, in effect, "I have a right to be here and here I will stay!"

Traditionally, the third temptation is always the sneaky, subtle temptation of pride. Whispering in Siddhartha's ear, Mara congratulated him on his spiritual growth, telling him that his insights and dedication were too profound for normal people to understand, and that it would be profitless to attempt to teach them to others. But Siddhartha resisted and conquered. At last, Mara left him alone.

With this spiritual victory over temptation, he passed through all stages of awareness. In a vision he saw all his previous incarnations and understood their connectedness, how they had brought him to this point in time and place. Now he sensed *Karma* at work—the guiding force that propels life forward.

More important, in a sudden intuitive leap, he grasped how to break out of *Samsara*, the wheel of life, death, and rebirth. He had finally found that for which he had been searching, even though he hadn't known what he was looking for. He achieved the goal of his quest. He became the Buddha, the Enlightened One.

(At this point, although the legends are silent, he probably went someplace to eat dinner, for he is never pictured as being thin and frail again.)

He called his insight the Dharma. It is simply this:

There is a Middle Way that leads between the poles of all opposites to the place beyond, wherein are embraced all dualities.

"Duality" means pair of opposites. Cold cannot exist except in comparison to heat, joy without the contrast of sorrow. One half of every pair of opposites is uncomfortable. The natural human tendency is to identify with that which is good, comfortable, or otherwise desirable. The Buddha saw this was impossible. Unless both poles of opposites are embraced, one cannot be content, because both poles are real and make up the fabric of life. To remain insulated from one pole or the other is to live an incomplete life.

Eventually, even if someone dwells in a palace, he or she must journey outside the walls to experience the reality that is comprised of life in all its totality. Denying or even ignoring death and sickness doesn't make them less real. All it creates is anxiety, because the human psyche knows they are inevitable.

What the Buddha came to understand is a profound psychological truth that has become a part of every culture on Earth. It is so common that we forget that Siddhartha was the first to put it into words and to frame it in a way that easily transcends culture and language.

What this means for us is that Merlin, too, understood this profound truth. Magic lies beyond the boundaries of duality. Sometimes, when it breaks into our material world, it must do its work by embracing both sides of duality. After all, both sides of reality make up the truth of our existence. We can't ignore one side, or hope that it will go away. Together they make up the fabric of life.

Could there have been a Judaism without the destruction of Jerusalem and the Babylonian captivity? Could there have been a Christianity without a crucifixion? Could Islam have come into existence without the slaughter of the Crusades?

The Merlin story becomes deathly serious at this point. We live in a hopelessly divided, destructive, and heart-breaking world that is also capable of great glory and good.

We're never going to legislate a perfect civilization into existence. We can't moralize our way through to justice and peace. No scientific invention will usher in Utopia. To bring about those ends, sometimes we need the messy, confusing, counter-intuitive work of magic.

In the meantime,
as soon as the king's absence was discovered at the siege,
his army unadvisedly made an assault upon the walls
and provoked the besieged count to a battle.
Acting as inconsiderately as they,
he sallied forth with his men, thinking with such a small
handful to oppose a powerful army.
But it happened that he was killed in the very first brunt of
the fight and had all his men routed.
After this bold attempt came messengers to Igerna,
with the news both of the duke's death
and of the event of the siege.
But when they saw the king in the likeness of the consul,
sitting close by her,
they were struck with shame and astonishment
at his safe arrival there,
whom they had left dead at the siege.
They were wholly ignorant of the miracles which Merlin
had wrought with his medicines.
The king therefore smiled at the news,
and embracing the countess, said to her:
"Your own eyes may convince you that I am not dead,
but alive.

But notwithstanding, the destruction of the town and the slaughter of my men is what very much grieves me, so that there is reason to fear the king's coming upon us and taking us in this place. To prevent which, I will go out to meet him and make my peace with him, for fear of a worse disaster." Accordingly, as soon as he was out of the town, he went to his army, and having put off the disguise of Gorlois, was now Uther Pendragon again. When he had a full relation made to him how matters had succeeded, he was sorry for the death of Gorlois, but rejoiced that Igerna was now at liberty to marry again. Then he returned to the town of Tintangel, which he took, and in it, what he impatiently wished for, Igerna herself. After this they continued to live together with much affection for each other, and had a son, whose name was Arthur.

In the end, we are left with a very unsatisfactory conclusion to what, up to now, has been a fascinating, one might even say heroic, swashbuckling tale. Only Merlin, it seems, accomplished anything good. He brought about the birth of the once and future king at precisely the right time. He was the only one to see the greater purpose that was being carried out.

Was he comfortable with the outcome? Yes. Did he approve of the process? As we shall soon see, probably not. But he was able to accept it. Although he lived within the confines of a world of dualism, he was somehow able to keep his balance by accepting both sides of the duality. He could live with right and wrong. He accepted both life and death. He recognized the needs of his ego but could subjugate those needs to the greater good. In the midst of the sordid schemes of a lustful king, he could still operate out of love. This was no easy task. Is it any wonder he needed magic to retain his sanity?

Let's recap the lessons he understood and practiced:

- **A spiritual force above and beyond duality is at work in the cosmos, and sometimes breaks through into human affairs. When it does, we call it magic. It isn't always pretty.**

- There is a Middle Way that leads between the poles of all opposites to the place beyond, wherein are embraced all dualities.

- We're never going to legislate a perfect civilization into existence. We can't moralize our way through to justice and peace. No scientific invention will usher in Utopia. To bring about those ends, sometimes we need the messy, confusing, counter-intuitive work of magic.

Thus it was that Arthur came to be born. Other stories tell the story of how he was raised, away from the royal household, in ignorance of his birth. Uther knew full well that people could count, and worried that they might become suspicious when Arthur was born so soon after the death of Gorlois and the subsequent royal marriage of Uther and Igerna. He was hoping for another son who could become king, instead of the royal bastard who would no doubt be considered Gorlois' son, not Uther's.

But magic has a way of sorting itself out in ways that we never suspect. It will have its way, whether we plan for it or not. Who would have ever considered that the way to the throne led through a magical sword?

THE TEXT

(From *Six Ballads About King Arthur*
Anonymous: 1881)

When Uther passed away, the realm fell in great jeopardy, for many wended to be king through might and bravery.

Then Merlin to the Archbishop of Canterbury went, and they together council took this evil to prevent.

Thus they agreed that every lord, on pain of curses deep, and every gentleman-at-arms a solemn tryst should keep.

On Christmas day, at London town, since Christ, as all do know, was then created Lord of all the kingdoms here below; so who should reign o'er England fair by miracle might show.

Some nobles made them passing clean from vice or crime, for fear their prayers might enter gracelessly, within Christ Jesus' ear.

Inside the church on Christmas day (It was St. Paul's, I ween), a mighty host of knights and lords and commoners is seen.

But ere they read the early mass or early matins sing, unto the Lord Archbishop there this startling news they bring:

"Outside, within the churchyard gate, near to the altar stone, there stands a large square marble slab with anvil perched thereon. And in the anvil, of pure steel a naked sword doth sit, of finest point, and all around are golden letters writ:

'Whoso from out this marble stone with his own powerful hand shall pluck this sword, he shall be Lord and King of all England.'"

The Lord Archbishop ordered then that none should touch the stone, but all within the church should pray until High Mass was done. And when all prayers were finished (this was his Grace's will), ten knights of stainless troth and fame should guard the sword from ill. That jousts and tournaments be held upon the New Year's Day, that all who willed their prowess try to pluck the sword away.

Thereto there flocked a gallant host of knights and ladies gay. Sir Ector brought young Arthur there, and his own son, Sir Kay.

But then befell a woeful chance. Sir Kay had lost his sword, in sooth, had left it at his home. Then uttered he this word: "O foster brother! Backward speed. Ride fast for love of me, and when thou reachest Ector's house, my sword bring back to me."

"That will I," said the gallant youth, riding away alone. But when he reached the castle gate he found the wardour gone, and all the inmates, great and small, off to the tournament. Baffled and wroth he turned his horse and to the churchyard went.

"Ten thousand pities 'twere," he said, "My dearest brother Kay should at the joust withouten sword appear in disarray."

Whereat he lighted from his horse, and tied it to the stile, while to the tent he bent his steps and loitered there awhile to see if the ten guards were there. He recked not that they went with all the world, both rich and poor, to the great tournament.

So when he found no knights were there, but to the jousting gone, lightly yet fierce the sword he seized and pulled it from the stone.

And to Sir Kay delivered it, who wist, as soon as seen, that 'twas the sword from out the stone. Then said, "Full well I ween I have the sword, and I must be the King of all Englànd.

But when he showed it to his sire Sir Ector gave command that to the church he should repair and swear upon the book how gat he then the sword. But he, fearing his sire's rebuke, told how his foster brother came when all the knights were gone, and light and fiercely plucked the sword from out the magic stone.

"Now try again," Sir Ector said; Whereat they all assayed, but none save Arthur there availed to sunder out the blade.

And thrice again he made assay, and thrice the sword came free. Sir Ector and Sir Kay fell down upon their bended knee.

"O father! Why," young Arthur said, "your homage pay to me?"

"Because that God has willed it so. Thou art no son of mine. 'Twas Merlin brought thee to my arms from some far nobler line. But, O my liege! for King thou art, wilt thou to mine and me, who nurtured thee and brought thee up, a gracious sovereign be?"

But Arthur wept and made great dole at what Sir Ector said, that he no sire or mother had, then sweetly answerèd:

"Else were I much to blame! I am beholden so to you, command me, and may God me help I will your bidding do."

"Sir," said Sir Ector, "I will ask no more than that of all the lands you govern, my son Kay be made the Seneschal."

Replied young Arthur, "That shall be; I here my promise give that none but he that office fill while he or I shall live."

Then happèd it that on Twelfth day the Barons all assay to pluck the sword, but none prevail save Arthur on that day.

Then waxed they wroth, and Candlemas was fixed for the assay, yet still no knight but Arthur could pluck the sword away.

Then at high feast of Eastertide, also at Pentecost, none but young Arthur loosed the sword—The knights their temper lost.

But when the Lord Archbishop came, all cried with one accord, "We will have Arthur for our King. God wills him for our lord."

And down on bended knee they fell to pay him homage due. And thus he won Excalibur and all fair England too.

Soon Scotland, and the North, and Wales, to him obeisance made, won by prowess of his knights and of his trusty blade.

Chapter 6: Merlin and the Sword

When Uther passed away, the realm fell in great jeopardy,
for many wended to be king through might and bravery.
Then Merlin to the Archbishop of Canterbury went,
and they together council took this evil to prevent.
Thus, they agreed that every lord, on pain of curses deep,
and every gentleman-at-arms a solemn tryst should keep.
On Christmas day, at London town,
since Christ, as all do know,
was then created Lord of all the kingdoms here below;
so who should reign o'er England fair
by miracle might show.
Some nobles made them passing clean from vice or crime,
for fear their prayers might enter gracelessly,
within Christ Jesus' ear.
Inside the church on Christmas day
(It was St. Paul's, I ween),
a mighty host of knights and lords and commoners is seen.
But ere they read the early mass or early matins sing,
unto the Lord Archbishop there
this startling news they bring:
"Outside, within the churchyard gate,

*near to the altar stone,
there stands a large square marble slab
with anvil perched thereon.
And in the anvil, of pure steel a naked sword doth sit,
of finest point, and all around are golden letters writ:
'Whoso from out this marble stone with his own powerful
hand shall pluck this sword,
he shall be Lord and King of all England.'*

In all of Arthurian lore, the most well-known story is undoubtedly the tale of the sword in the stone. When Excalibur, from the French spelling, or Caladfwlch in Welsh, or Geoffrey of Monmouth's Caliburn, was pulled from the stone, it produced an iconic image that will probably be remembered forever. But there is a lot going on here that is often missed by those who are reading only for the entertainment value of a great story. "*Whoso from out this marble stone with his own powerful hand shall pluck this sword, he shall be Lord and King of all England.*" What a powerful picture!

But let's look a little deeper into the story by analyzing the symbolism and mythic motifs.

First, consider the backdrop. Merlin, priest of the old earth-based religion, meets with none other than the Christian Archbishop of Canterbury in order to come up with a plan to save a realm that had fallen *in great jeopardy, for many wended to be king through might and bravery.*

The old religion and the new now met to save a future that hung in the balance. The fateful day it all took place was none other than that amalgamation called Christmas, a Christian feast day festooned with pagan symbols. It marked the birthday of the Christ, while celebrating the event with evergreen trees, Yule logs, and mistletoe. It held up the image of a virgin queen, visited by astrologers from the mysterious far-away east, who were following a star. Even in this day and age, if you arrived on Planet Earth from a distant galaxy, knowing nothing about the local customs, you would have trouble determining the true nature of Christmas. Imagine your confusion if you were told that the birthday of the Prince of Peace, who told his followers to give everything away and follow him, was marked by counting down the number of shopping days until the big event, and the most popular gifts were toys consisting of gun-wielding robots and violent video games.

Your confusion could easily be forgiven. Even true believers seldom get their minds around the dichotomy of the season.

So in this tale, when the ultimate feat is accomplished, and Excalibur is freed from the stone, it takes place within a climate of Paganism and Christianity, Earth-based religion and Heaven-centered faith, all within the context of the twin poles of duality, working together to save a kingdom from its own ego-centered destruction.

The truce wouldn't last. But at least at the outset, it was hopeful.

Notice also how the story pairs the two religions opposite each other in their traditional settings. The church is meeting inside, behind closed doors, in a sacred space filled with icons and images. The pagan altar is outside in the open air. We couldn't ask for a more obvious duality. The original religion of Eden had by this time moved indoors, towards its ultimate destiny in the New Jerusalem, "coming down out of heaven from God," as Revelation 21 so aptly describes it.

In this story we are witnessing a poetic version of the original split between the earth-based religion of the ancients, celebrated in oak groves and mountain sides, and the heaven-centered religion of the modern world, celebrated indoors with the latest technology. The split has only widened over time.

Quite a few years ago I attended a three-day, statewide gathering of a major Protestant denomination. Hundreds of people met together to discuss church business, worship together, renew old ties, and hold workshops around the theme of God and Ecology. Liturgies had been prepared that drew from many biblical verses which pointed to discovering God in nature. Some nationally known speakers even went so far as to prick the consciences of what was predominately a group of retired, upper-middle-class, churchgoing nature lovers who wouldn't even think of throwing a soda can out of the car window. It all seemed very hopeful.

Nevertheless, I was troubled throughout the entire weekend. The bulk of the people at that meeting were what I privately call "greenhouse" ecologists. That term requires some explanation.

I have been an outdoorsman most of my adult life. When I was younger, I would habitually take as long as a week off, in both spring and fall, to go into the woods and live off the land. I mean that very literally. I wouldn't take any food with me. All I had was a rifle or bow and arrow, perhaps a fishing rod, a hunting knife, and a sleeping bag or blanket. I would forage for my food, and if I couldn't hunt, fish, or gather up some supper, I went hungry. Some of the best spiritual moments of my life were spent eating roast woodchuck, cooked over an open fire, served up with some roots or berries, accompanied by pine needle tea laced with wild mint.

I have experienced the sublime, but also know firsthand about things like mosquitoes and black flies. The great outdoors is a beautiful place, but I think we ought to find the guy who invented the screened-in porch and award him the Nobel Prize. I have donated lots of money to groups ranging from the Sierra Club to Ducks Unlimited, and have volunteered many, many hours to the Appalachian Trail Club and local outdoors organizations. When I talk about ecology and the beauty of God in nature, I speak from an intimate knowledge and a lot of experience spent actually living outdoors.

That brings us to "greenhouse" ecologists. Because of all the gardening I've done, I have learned about hardening off plants before they can be placed outside. When you start tomato seedlings, for instance, from seed, in the greenhouse, they look beautiful and prolific, as long as they remain in their controlled environment. But if you take them right outside and plant them in the garden, exposed to the sun, wind, rain, heat, cold, and draught, they wilt and, usually, die. The real outdoors is too much for them. They simply can't take it. They need to experience the wild outdoors in small doses before they are ready.

People are like that. We love the outdoors as long as we stand in climate-controlled comfort and look at it through the window. But to actually walk out into a range of desert mountains, or canoe into a mosquito infested swamp? That's another story!

Our so-called "primitive" ancestors had the skills, and derived a healthy spiritual understanding of their place in nature. We don't. This is the twenty-first century. Most people just don't have that kind of experience to draw on. A large part of urban America frames ecological issues in a completely different way than those of us whose understanding of backcountry is forged well away from maintained trails and officially sanctioned campgrounds.

All this was rumbling about in my mind that weekend as I entered a beautiful church, full of the latest technology, that stood about one hundred yards from a beautiful beach located right on the Gulf of Mexico. We saw a gorgeous Power Point presentation, featuring pictures of planet Earth. The music consisted of aboriginal flutes and synthesized strings, earth drums and midi-track percussion.

As the light dimmed for the production, I became aware that we were most definitely meeting in a church sanctuary. "Sanctuary" means a place of refuge. It consisted of safe, secure, surrounding walls. Even the light was filtered by beautiful stained-glass windows. No natural light for us! The only complaint people had was that the air conditioning made the place a little cool. Some people felt the need for a light sweater.

As picture morphed into picture, we learned about the necessity to do two things. First of all, we needed to love, protect, and care for Mother Earth. Second, we needed to spread the word to others. Remember those two things. They will come back to haunt us in a few paragraphs.

One way, we were told, to experience the great outdoors that was being ravaged by development even as we met, was to perform an elaborate ritual in our churches. It consisted of obtaining sawdust from a local building supply store, and then bringing it home to our congregations, along with sheets of plastic and biodegradable paint. Then we were taught how to make what was, in effect, a copy of a Navaho sand painting. Young and old could be involved in planning the design, "painting" it on the sawdust which was spread on the plastic sheet, and then dancing together in celebratory mourning for the loss of trees and the natural world, when developers raise their ugly heads. The dancing, of course, ruined the painting, so after the ritual was complete, we were all instructed to gather up the sawdust, take it home, and use it as mulch for our gardens.

My wife and I just looked at each other in disbelief. We didn't know whether to laugh or cry. We were sitting in an air-conditioned sanctuary, cut off by four walls that eliminated everything natural, looking at plastic flowers on the walls, listening to digitized music, while looking at pictures of Mother Earth. Filtered air, filtered light, filtered music, and enhanced pictures. The ritual we were taught, which was designed to help celebrate nature, consisted of plastic sheets, construction wastes, and chemically treated paint. Fossil fuels galore had been burned up in driving to this event. And the service ended with the singing of a hymn extolling the fact that this is God's world.

That night my wife and I took a walk on the beach rather than attend the evening workshops. The Gulf of Mexico was less than a hundred yards away from the front door of the church. When the sun sank into the ocean, I happened to glance up the beach to the north and was struck by a scene that I will never forget. As far as the eye could see there were people standing quietly, looking in unison toward the west. All we heard was the sound of waves and wind. (That is, if we chose to ignore the sound of the traffic on the state highway.) When the sun finally set, without anyone saying "Amen," with no organ postlude, and no minister to pronounce a benediction, the beach crowd (pagans all, for a moment, and proud of it!) completed their rite, turned, nodded a few quiet greetings, and slowly went home.

We had participated in a ritual as old as the human race. We had experienced beauty, and stood in awe and wonder at a riveting sight of unmitigated mystery. We had, together, contemplated the meaning of life. "Beauty is truth, and truth beauty—that is all ye know on earth, and all ye need to know," wrote the English poet John Keats. And the gathered congregation said, each in his or her own way, "Amen!"

The next night, again safely ensconced in the cool sanctuary, surrounded by beautiful music and meaningful liturgy, we heard again about the need to experience God in nature and to spread the word to others. For the entire time the service was going on I could think of only one thing. Right outside the door, not one hundred yards away, stood hundreds of people, many of them non-church-going people, who were having their own worship service. I wanted to shout at the top of my voice, "Why don't we just open the doors? There's the beauty—the real thing—unfiltered! There are the people! They're only a few steps away!"

But, of course, I'm a well-adjusted, fully accredited, ordained minister. I kept my mouth shut.

The people in that congregation no doubt considered themselves religious conservationists. And, to a great extent, they were. They wouldn't have been at a meeting like that unless they cared. But their lives were lived on a level of affluence of which former generations could not have even dreamed. Neither Napoleon nor Queen Elizabeth ever kicked back in the evening to watch, at their leisure, a Masterpiece Theater rerun. We moderns, however, take such luxuries for granted—so much so that we are hardly aware of the fact that complete climate control is ours at the flick of a switch. What would Peter the Great, in all his regal splendor, have paid for that?

By the same token, the folks out on the beach were probably not aware that a group of people only a few steps away would have welcomed them warmly and delighted in sharing stories of spirituality with them. Many of the beachgoers no doubt had only negative things to say about their previous church experiences. Statistically, any group of people contains a small percentage of those who feel burned by institutional religion. This group was, no doubt, average.

What if both congregations could have reframed their cultural bias to include a healthy respect for their counterparts? What if the modern Merlins could have met with the contemporary Archbishops? Could a bridge have been built between them?

Remember that I am using these two groups as metaphors. I am well aware that there were probably some believers on the beach, as well as pagans in the pews. But when viewed metaphorically, the two groups become a valuable way to picture disparate groups of today's society who have long since given up even the effort to see another point of view. Nevertheless, our spiritual social health depends on doing just that. We simply must learn to see other points of view while refraining from spiritual pride in our own. It's all about reframing.

With this as a backdrop, we can continue to look at the symbols of the story.

The sword, of course, is a universal symbol of masculine power. Sigmund Freud had a field day talking about that. But masculine power is neither good nor bad in and of itself. It is a complimentary *Yang* to Female energy's *Yin*. It is how it is used that is important.

But notice that, at the beginning of the story, masculine power is held firmly in check by Mother Earth.

It is safely ensconced and protected. Only the worthy may free it from the Mother's embrace. Through the miracle of birth, everyone, whether they are good or bad, saints or sinners, redemptive or wicked, male or female, proceeds from the mother. Then, freed from her embrace, the birth canal becomes our entrance into life. We are pulled from nature's womb and enter into a world that, ideally at least, consists of perfect balance. Regardless of our gender, Yin and Yang are complimentary.

If we look ahead for a minute, and anticipate what is to come, we will see that when the sword has served its purpose, when it has fulfilled its function, it is returned to the Mother, but in a different form.

We are looking at Merlin's story, of course, but the Arthurian legend, as recorded by Mallory, tells us that when Arthur lies dying on the field, a victim of a mortal wound delivered by Mordred during the Battle of Camlann, he instructs Sir Bedivere to throw the sword into the nearby lake. A woman's arm rises up out of the water and grabs the sword by the hilt, taking it back down again into the embrace of the Lady of the Lake, who served the Earth Mother. Thus, balance is restored. Masculine stone defers to feminine water.

But in the interim, things easily spin out of control. We have only to look at the ecological havoc huge man-toys have inflicted on the earth today to see that truth. In our generation, the unworthy have figured out how to pull the "sword," unbridled masculine energy, out of the stone and wield it with impunity. The result is unthinkably horrific. We have despoiled the whole planet. Earth and Heaven have been seemingly sundered forever.

If ever there was the need for an Arthur, who can wield masculine energy with the pure strength of egoic innocence, it is now. But the power behind Arthur was Merlin and his magic, and we have stopped believing in such things. So, because we have allowed real magic to atrophy through our disbelief, we have doomed ourselves to our own feeble efforts and futile attempts to control something that is much bigger and more powerful than ourselves and our perceptual experience.

The Lord Archbishop ordered then
that none should touch the stone,
but all within the church should pray
until High Mass was done.
And when all prayers were finished

(this was his Grace's will),
ten knights of stainless troth and fame
should guard the sword from ill.
That jousts and tournaments be held
upon the New Year's Day,
that all who willed their prowess try
to pluck the sword away.
Thereto there flocked a gallant host
of knights and ladies gay.
Sir Ector brought young Arthur there,
and his own son, Sir Kay.
But then befell a woeful chance.
Sir Kay had lost his sword,
in sooth, had left it at his home.
Then uttered he this word: "O foster brother!
Backward speed. Ride fast for love of me,
and when thou reachest Ector's house,
my sword bring back to me."
"That will I," said the gallant youth, riding away alone.
But when he reached the castle gate
he found the wardour gone,
and all the inmates, great and small,
off to the tournament.
Baffled and wroth he turned his horse

and to the churchyard went.

"Ten thousand pities 'twere," he said,

"My dearest brother Kay

should at the joust withouten sword appear in disarray."

Whereat he lighted from his horse, and tied it to the stile,

while to the tent he bent his steps

and loitered there awhile

to see if the ten guards were there.

He recked not that they went with all the world,

both rich and poor, to the great tournament.

So when he found no knights were there,

but to the jousting gone,

lightly yet fierce the sword he seized

and pulled it from the stone.

Ego, in its purest form, is called innocence. Neither Merlin nor the archbishop were capable of true innocence. Although they arose from two different religious systems and world views, they had both seen and experienced too much. The old Druid and the professional clergyman were no doubt, by this time in their careers, seasoned veterans of the infighting that persists in any worldly culture.

Meanwhile, however, Arthur, in complete innocence, is trying to do the right thing. He doesn't yet realize who he is or what he is capable of. His only concern is to do what is required of him.

Eventually, seemingly by chance, he is guided to free the sword, thus placing him on the path of his destiny. Of all the powerful men in the kingdom that day, he is the only one who wanted to pull the sword from the stone for someone else, rather than himself. Becoming king was the farthest thing from his mind. He wanted only to help his brother. That is real innocence. And, in his purity of heart, he was capable of doing something no one else could do.

President Harry Truman once said, "It is amazing what you can accomplish if you do not care who gets the credit."

Truer words were never spoken.

But if good deeds done in innocence are observed and recorded by observant witnesses, they can go on to inspire and effect great change for the good.

And to Sir Kay delivered it, who wist, as soon as seen, that 'twas the sword from out the stone.

Then said, "Full well I ween
I have the sword, and I must be the King of all Englànd.
But when he showed it to his sire Sir Ector gave command
that to the church he should repair
and swear upon the book how gat he then the sword.
But he, fearing his sire's rebuke,
told how his foster brother came
when all the knights were gone,
and light and fiercely plucked the sword
from out the magic stone.
"Now try again," Sir Ector said;
Whereat they all assayed, but none save Arthur there
availed to sunder out the blade.
And thrice again he made assay,
and thrice the sword came free.
Sir Ector and Sir Kay fell down upon their bended knee.
"O father! Why," young Arthur said,
"your homage pay to me?"
"Because that God has willed it so.
Thou art no son of mine.
'Twas Merlin brought thee to my arms
from some far nobler line.
But, O my liege! for King thou art,
wilt thou to mine and me,

who nurtured thee and brought thee up,
a gracious sovereign be?"
But Arthur wept and made great dole
at what Sir Ector said,
that he no sire or mother had, then sweetly answerèd:
"Else were I much to blame! I am beholden so to you,
command me,
and may God me help I will your bidding do."
"Sir," said Sir Ector, "I will ask no more
than that of all the lands you govern,
my son Kay be made the Seneschal."
Replied young Arthur,
"That shall be; I here my promise give
that none but he that office fill while he or I shall live."
Then happèd it that on Twelfth day the Barons all assay
to pluck the sword, but none prevail
save Arthur on that day.
Then waxed they wroth,
and Candlemas was fixed for the assay,
yet still no knight but Arthur could pluck the sword away.
Then at high feast of Eastertide, also at Pentecost,
none but young Arthur loosed the sword—
The knights their temper lost.
But when the Lord Archbishop came,

*all cried with one accord,
"We will have Arthur for our King.
God wills him for our lord."*

Now the truth is revealed and Arthur discovers his real identity. On the outside he is merely a young man, similar to all others. Inside, he is a king.

Both the Old and New Testaments of the Bible, using the words of a Jewish psalmist and Jesus himself, quote the same universal truth: "Know ye not that ye are gods?"

Arthur lives within each one of us. But, like the innocent youth of the old tales, we are ignorant of our own parentage. Only Merlin knows the truth. This leads us to an important conclusion:

If we don't know who we are, how can we possibly act like we should?

Arthur's innocence and pureness of heart allowed him access to two worlds—the world of the spirit and the world of the material. That's how we were intended to operate in this perception realm. We are not without resources in our direst hour of need. But the fact that we have turned our back on the energy stemming from Mother Earth herself means that we have, by our own hand, cut off the best source of power available to help us through life's twists and turns. Is it any wonder we struggle so, and fall victim to so much emotional turmoil?

The story goes on to remind us that when we avail ourselves of the power that is our birthright, people take notice.

And down on bended knee
they fell to pay him homage due.
And thus he won Excalibur and all fair England too.
Soon Scotland, and the North, and Wales,
to him obeisance made,
won by prowess of his knights and of his trusty blade.

It is ironic that this incident marks a watershed moment in our history. It is one of the last times the inherent power of earth energy is acknowledged by the political elite. We have pulled many swords out of many stones in our time. We have split the atom and released male energy in its fullest, sword-like strength. But we have not done so with the innocence of Arthur. As a result, we have paid the price.

But there is hope. Relatively recently in our experience have we learned how to peer beneath the power of the sword and discover the world of the quantum. And what have we found? Magic! Merlin still lives in the equations of those who seek the real truth about how the world works.

Underlying everything, hidden magic is the source of all that is!

And therein lies our hope, as long as we remember that true magic can only be used by the pure of heart, who are innocent and free from selfish ego. Arthur, the innocent youth, lives within each of us, and longs to free the sword in the stone.

Once again, let's recap the lessons:

- **In this story we are witnessing a poetic version of the original split between the earth-based religion of the ancients, celebrated in oak groves and** mountain sides, and the heaven-centered religion of the modern world, celebrated indoors with the latest technology.

- The split has only widened over time.

- If we don't know who we are, how can we possibly act like we should?

- Underlying everything, hidden magic is the source of all that is!

THE TEXT

From *The Life of Merlin* (*Vita Merlini*): Geoffrey of Monmouth
Translated by **John Jay Parry**
[1925, copyright not renewed]

Merlin the Briton was now held famous in the world. He was a king and prophet. To the proud people of the South Welsh he gave laws, and to the chieftains he prophesied the future. But in time he departed secretly and fled to the forest, not wishing to be seen. He entered the wood and rejoiced to lie hidden under the ash trees. He marveled at the wild beasts feeding on the grass of the glades. He chased after them and sometimes flew past them. He lived on the roots of grasses and on the grass, on the fruit of the trees, and on the mulberries of the thicket. He became a sylvan man just as though devoted to the woods. Hidden like a wild animal, he remained buried in the woods, found by no one of his kindred.

On the very summit of a certain mountain there was a fountain, surrounded on every side by hazel bushes and thick with shrubs. There Merlin seated himself, and thence *through all the woods he watched the wild animals running and playing.*

Chapter 7: Merlin and Wilderness Wisdom

Merlin the Briton was now held famous in the world.
He was a king and prophet.
To the proud people of the South Welsh he gave laws,
and to the chieftains he prophesied the future.

Once you anoint a king and prove to the world that you are a magician to be respected, you can pretty much call your own shots. After Arthur rose to prominence, Merlin could have retired to a life of ease. He had some busy work to take care of first, but to the people of his native Wales, he was now THE MAN.

A life of prominence, however, was not in his nature. As it turns out, he had no taste for the limelight. That's where ego dwells, not magic.

But in time he departed secretly and fled to the forest,
not wishing to be seen.
He entered the wood and rejoiced to lie

> hidden under the ash trees.
> He marveled at the wild beasts
> feeding on the grass of the glades.
> He chased after them and sometimes flew past them.
> He lived on the roots of grasses and on the grass,
> on the fruit of the trees,
> and on the mulberries of the thicket.
> He became a sylvan man
> just as though devoted to the woods.
> Hidden like a wild animal, he remained
> buried in the woods, found by no one of his kindred.

Instead of politics, he chose a life of spirituality. He became a woods hermit. The ego-driven intrigue of court and conference hall left him cold. He decided for wisdom instead of worldly knowledge.

I can relate. I've written about this in some of my other books, but it bears repeating because I think it's important for people of today to, in their latter years especially, break the hold of modern life with its incessant, ego-driven inspired demand to stay in touch through constant social media and noise. Those are the things that I believe will destroy us in the end. Maybe it's already too late. Lifetime habits are so tough to break that most people I talk to about this problem simply refuse to acknowledge that it even exists.

Let's face it, my friends. We face a crisis of the spirit today, and it all stems from the fact that there is more to life than increasing its speed.

We came to being and evolved within the energy of Mother Earth. Apart from her we cannot find our true essence. We need to slow down, quiet our heart, and learn to listen. That takes time and peace. Nothing short of that will do. In this sense, the ancients knew what we have forgotten. This is the central problem of the modern world.

Henry David Thoreau said it this way: "I went to the woods because I wished to live deliberately, to front only the essential facts of life, and see if I could not learn what it had to teach, and not, when I came to die, discover that I had not lived."

When I retired from active ministry and teaching back in 2009, I decided to take Thoreau seriously. I wanted to live, using his word, "deliberately." This was more retreat than retirement. I didn't want to spend a few days, or even a month or two, seeking the face of God. I wanted to spend years, if that's what it took, to see what would happen.

AARP magazine teaches senior citizens that we need to stay engaged, surrounded by friends and family. Otherwise, they say, we will get depressed.

Well, they are right. When you break lifelong habits and completely change your manner of relating to the world, depression is one stage of the journey. It's not the only stage, but I won't kid you—it happens.

I can say, however, that if you have the spiritual inclination, and either money in the bank or the willingness to cut your expenses to the absolute bone, which is what I had to do, it's worth it. When you decide to live away from the distraction other human beings might impose on you, and decide to confront the essence of spirit, you essentially begin to live in a state of meditation. It will not be easy, but it will change your life.

Most retired ministers stay somehow involved with the church in one way or another. Many professors become part-time teachers. That was not the direction I took. I wanted to experience God—however God would reveal himself, or herself, or itself.

The key word is "experience." I've said this a hundred times in a hundred different ways. I'm not talking about "knowing about," "studying" or "reading up on." To me, if God is real, spiritual peek-a-boo just won't cut it. I have no interest in a God who, in the words of the Bible, created humans "in His image," and then left them to fend for themselves without any apparent means of support.

Because of my passion—some have gone so far as to call it an obsession—I can finally freely admit that religion, even my own, has never been really satisfying for me. God was only exciting when I was learning something new, and I never found one way of thinking or practicing religion that explained and neatly codified all that could be known about God.

After a long life in ministry and academia, I had earned the right to call myself an expert, and retire into a life of contentment and pleasure. But I did not intend to give spirituality a rest. I chose instead to wrestle with God, like Jacob of old, saying, "I will not let you go until you bless me!"

That's what Merlin chose. "*He became a sylvan man ... Hidden like a wild animal, he remained buried in the woods, found by no one of his kindred.*"

Thus was born the legend of Merlin the Hermit and his famous well, sought by so many, and found by no one. At least, not yet.

*On the very summit of a certain mountain
there was a fountain,
surrounded on every side by hazel bushes
and thick with shrubs.
There Merlin seated himself,
and thence through all the woods
he watched the wild animals running and playing.*

Is it possible to find a rich spiritual life in the hustle and bustle of activity, with its constant noise and distractions?

Probably. But I wouldn't know. I couldn't do it. Maybe you can. Obviously, Merlin couldn't.

I suspect, though, that those who won't even *consider* the possibility of retreating back to nature for extended periods, and still want to undertake spiritual growth, have a problem. If you suspect I'm talking about you, it might be that, without your knowing it, you have become addicted to modern life. Your ego, in keeping with so many people today, may live in terrible fear of being alone with itself, and having nothing or no one to interact with except its nemesis, the peace and unity of the Source.

Alcoholics or drug addicts need to first admit that they have a problem before they can be helped. Sometimes that only happens when they try to cut themselves off from the source of their addiction, and discover they cannot. So, try this, if you harbor doubts about yourself. Unplug. Turn off your computer and your smart phone. Turn off your TV and radio. Don't do it for a day or so. Anyone can find the self-control to last that long. Try it for at least a week.

Can you spend a week with no entertainment, other than yourself and your inner being, perhaps aided only a good book or two? If not, you will never even *find* your soul, let alone become *comfortable* with it.

Your *soul* is your eternal "You," not your ego. And the simple truth is that most people in this hectic and distracting world have ignored that truth, to the point where they utterly panic if they even have to spend an hour in a doctor's waiting room with no hand-held device to occupy their time.

Our grandparents spent hours alone, perhaps working in a cornfield, or building something, with no music or talking to distract them. They hitched up the horses and rode ten miles to town to go to a store, without ever saying a word. They were alone with their thoughts.

I've hiked for miles on the Appalachian Trail with no cell phone. Last time I walked a portion of that famous old pathway through the eastern woods, I found people who stopped at the top of a mountain, not to admire the view, but because they got great reception on their smart phone.

Is it any wonder we are wound up so tight these days?

Merlin could have chosen a life of sophisticated responsibility. Instead, he chose the path of a wisdom tradition that sought seclusion, instead of noise and activity.

It is no accident that saints and gurus of old went out into the desert, or up into a mountain retreat, when they sought wisdom and spiritual growth. That's the only place you can find it.

When you find yourself stretched too thin, and spread out like too little butter over too much bread, remember Merlin's example.

- We came to being and evolved within the energy of Mother Earth. Apart from her we cannot find our true essence.

- We need to slow down, quiet our heart, and learn to listen. That takes time and peace. Nothing short of that will do.

- In this sense, the ancients knew what we have forgotten. This is the central problem of the modern world.

Retreats, however, cannot last forever. Important as it is to remove ourselves from the hectic pace of life, there comes a time, if we are going to be of service to humanity, that we have to go back to the throngs, and impart what we have learned. That's why authors write books, and poets publish poetry. A musician needs to practice, alone and hard. It's a lonely craft. But what good is music if it remains unheard? He or she needs to perform in public, or the music is forever stilled.

That's why, eventually, Merlin had to leave his beloved retreat and return to the city. The once and future king needed a city set on a hill. It could not happen without magic.

THE TEXT

From *Idylls of the King*: Alfred, Lord Tennyson

Spoken by the gatekeeper of Camelot in Gareth and Lynette

"And, as thou sayest, Camelot is enchanted, son, for there is nothing in it as it seems, saving the King; tho' some there be that hold the King a shadow, and the city real."

From *Idylls of the King*: Alfred, Lord Tennyson

Spoken by Arthur to Guinevere in Guinevere

"But I was first of all the kings who drew the knighthood-errant of this realm and all the realms together under me, their Head, in that fair order of my Table Round at Camelot, a glorious company, the flower of men, to serve as model for the mighty world and be the fair beginning of a time."

From *Avalon of the Heart*: Van Morrison

I came upon the enchanted vale, down by the viaducts of my dreams.
Near Camelot hangs the tale of the enchanted vale.
In the upper room there the cup does stand.
In the upper room down by Avalon.

Chapter 8: Merlin and the City

And, as thou sayest, Camelot is enchanted, son,
for there is nothing in it as it seems, saving the King;
tho' some there be that hold the King a shadow,
and the city real.

One way to understand the history of our civilization is to view it, for better or for worse, as a journey from the wilderness to the city. We began as hunter/gatherers, who moved from place to place, following the wild game that fed and nurtured us. After many millennia, perhaps two or three hundred thousand years, we learned, while still moving around in search of fresh grazing ground, to domesticate animals. Then came the invention of agriculture, forcing us to settle in one spot while the crops grew and flourished until the harvest. From this last practice grew the birth of cities, which featured specialized labor practices, political systems, formal religion, armies for protection and expansion, and all the rest. The series of changes is sometimes called "the march of civilization." At least, this is the pattern usually taught today.

In the first few chapters of the Bible, the book of Genesis outlines the procedure. If we read the biblical story as a multi-millennial era, rather than an event that took place over a few days, it offers some ancient insight. It says that we began the journey in nature—specifically, a paradise named Eden. From there we slowly began the evolutionary, revolutionary, developments that led to the urban sprawl of today.

Take this summary from Genesis 4 for instance:

City Building:

Cain went out from the LORD's presence and lived in the land of Nod, east of Eden. Cain made love to his wife, and she became pregnant and gave birth to Enoch. Cain was then building a city, and he named it after his son Enoch.

Population Expansion:

To Enoch was born Irad, and Irad was the father of Mehujael, and Mehujael was the father of Methushael, and Methushael was the father of Lamech ... men began to multiply upon the earth.

Development of Controversial Social Customs:

> *Lamech married two women, one named Adah and the other Zillah.*

Animal Husbandry:

> *Adah gave birth to Jabal; he was the father of those who live in tents and raise livestock.*

The Arts:

> *His brother's name was Jubal; he was the father of all who play stringed instruments and pipes.*

Industry:

> *Zillah also had a son, Tubal-Cain, who forged all kinds of tools out of bronze and iron. Tubal-Cain's sister was Naamah.*

Grit in the Civilization Machine:

> *Lamech said to his wives, "Adah and Zillah, listen to me; wives of Lamech, hear my words. I have killed a man for wounding me, a young man for injuring me. If Cain is avenged seven times, then Lamech seventy-seven times."*

Religion:

>*At that time people began to call on the name of the LORD.*

These verses form a pretty good description of what most history books teach today. Granted, differing views are now coming to light, as modern scholars uncover new facts and form new theories about social development, but the journey from nature to city is fairly well laid out.

The process that began in Genesis, the first book of the Bible, comes to fulfilment in Revelation, the final book:

>*I saw the Holy City, the new Jerusalem, coming down out of heaven from God, prepared as a bride beautifully dressed for her husband. And I heard a loud voice from the throne saying, "Look! God's dwelling place is now among the people, and he will dwell with them. They will be his people, and God himself will be with them and be their God. He will wipe every tear from their eyes. There will be no more death, or mourning, or crying, or pain, for the old order of things has passed away."*

He who was seated on the throne said, "I am making everything new!" Then he said, "Write this down, for these words are trustworthy and true."

He said to me: "It is done. I am the Alpha and the Omega, the Beginning and the End.

Revelation 21:2-6

According to this account, humankind began in a wilderness garden, rooted and grounded in the earth, one with nature, which God had declared "very good." The story ends in a glorious city that comes down from the skies above. It pictures a marriage between Gaia, the Earth Mother, and a divine "Father" God who lives in Heaven. *"Look! God's dwelling place is now among the people, and he will dwell with them. They will be his people, and God himself will be with them, and be their God."*

This is a uniquely Christian view of human "progress." But don't forget—Christians wrote the first Merlin accounts. Their prejudice no doubt peeks through from time to time.

Whatever the case, the Merlin story follows a similar path. Merlin, the man of the sylvan woods, ends his public career by building the kingly city remembered as Camelot. "Magic" lives in the wild. Arthur, the Christian king, will henceforth rule from a city: *"And, as thou sayest, Camelot is enchanted."*

But all is not as it appears, *"for there is nothing in it as it seems, saving the King."* In other words, in a very meaningful way, life in the city is an illusion. It is not entirely authentic. Its attractions appear as bright baubles of convenience and ease, but those comforts come with a price. In the city, magic all too easily bows to technology and convenience.

Magic thrives in contemplative, meditative, silence. It is usually conducted in quiet ritual, decently and in order. The city, however, is full of bustling, noisy, clamorous confusion.

The city offers socially-controlled predictability and rules. Nature harbors the unknown, with fairies and elves potentially behind every bush, haunting every glade. It is not a coincidence that most every hero's journey begins with an encounter in the wildwood.

The city utters a clarion call, but we must be careful, *"for there is nothing in it as it seems."* Cities, which, by extension, mean civilization, are, at their root, an illusion. They offer the safety of comfort and convenience, for instance. But if the electrical grid that powers them ever breaks down due to a catastrophe of some sort, or if the choreographed dance that keeps them moving is hit by a labor union strike or pandemic of some sort, the only ones who will not be troubled or inconvenienced are those who live in the remote rain forests or far-flung deserts; who spend their days unaware that such places even exist. Cities seem to be a bustling hive of lively company, wherein people are surrounded by others. But everyone knows they can really be places of loneliness and depression.

Never the less, they are enticing. Right after World War I, a popular song in America asked the pertinent question, "How Ya Gonna Keep 'em Down on the Farm (After They've Seen Paree?)" The reason for the ditty's popularity was more than the fact that it featured a catchy, bouncy, melody. It raised a concerning issue. GIs, straight from the American heartland, had been exposed to a European sophistication and civilization far more glamorous than most of them had ever seen. And the truth is that many of them *didn't* go back to the farm. They moved to New York, Chicago, Detroit, and a boom town called Los Vegas, that soon began to flourish in the Nevada desert They swelled the population of places called Hollywood and Los Angeles, where it was believed that there might be something interesting about a new form of entertainment called moving pictures.

These burgeoning cities all offered promise, and even a little magic. But it was contrived magic, based on technological prowess. They sucked people in by the millions, but "nothing was as it seemed." It was a superficial magic—which eventually turned into virtual magic. "*Some there be that hold the King a shadow, and the city real.*" Others, like Merlin, knew better.

Still, the march of progress, if that was what it was, continued. At first, it seemed to work, because the intentions of the king and others of good will were just and true. Arthur said it like this:

But I was first of all the kings who drew the knighthood-
errant of this realm and all the realms together under me,
their Head, in that fair order of my
Table Round at Camelot, a glorious company,
the flower of men,
to serve as model for the mighty world

and be the fair beginning of a time.

There would have been no Camelot, and no Arthur, without Merlin. There would have been no civilization, at least as we know it, without nature magic. That was the world into which we were born and developed our first, and authentic, identity. We spent two or three hundred thousand years there before we developed the relatively new and "improved" idea of the metropolis, about 10,000 years ago at most. In ancient Anatolia, in Sumeria and Egypt, in China and India, in South and Central America, cities grew to dominate our identity.

Alas, however, in a supreme bit of irony, Camelot, city of the king, became lost to history. No one knows for sure if it even ever existed, let alone exactly where it might have been located. But the legend lived on. The illusion lived on. In the 1967 movie *Camelot*, a song written by Frederick Loewe best summed it up:

Don't let it be forgot, that once there was a spot
For one brief shining moment that was known as Camelot.

All this points to an insightful conclusion that can be drawn about the city on a hill, a "civilized," "Christian," wonder, built by a pagan wizard who lived in the woods:

Much of what we call civilization is an illusion—a thin veneer, floating on the surface of a much deeper reality. Beneath this so-called "civilized" veneer, painted by monks centuries ago, lies a deeply pagan system of belief that refuses to go away. The values of "Christian" Camelot were thus formed by pagan, shamanic, pre-Druidic formulations, that refuse to be compromised. They are with us still.

This is a very important insight. If civilization is a thin veil of illusion, it's important that we recognize it as such.

Ireland, historically, was the last bastion of ancient Celtic religion before, if legend is true, St. Patrick converted it to Christianity. Since then, the Emerald Isle has been known for its staunch adherence to Catholicism. But many historians, including those from Ireland, point out that Christianity in Ireland, and in many other Celtic strongholds, was not so much a deep well as much as a thin surface, that was supported by the depths of paganism. Many pagan customs found their way into the new belief system. Yule logs at Christmas, fertility symbols, such as rabbits and eggs at Easter, even the dates utilized for high holy days, and formal prayers offered to certain pagan deities such as St. Nicholas, who seemed to have obtained an ecclesiastical "baptism," are still paramount in the Christian religion.

The early Christian monks who first wrote about Merlin may have outwardly followed the principles of their religion in claiming that the Christian Arthur and his Knights of the Round Table followed the practices of their faith, but that faith seems buttressed by a deep underlayment of paganism. And at the bottom of it all lies Merlin. He is the architect. He is the founder. It was he who built Camelot, and his magic undergirds the whole thing.

Thus:

When we read about Camelot, we experience a sea change in the Merlin story. Camelot is about transitions—from Paganism to Christianity, from nature to the city,

from wildness to civilization, from magic to so-called rationality.

Perhaps there is no greater illustration of this principle than to examine the quest for the Holy Grail. Similar religious icons permeate paganism. They are emblems of magic that bless their possessors with special gifts of healing, strength, and wisdom. It was from Camelot that, one by one, the knights put aside their ego-driven thirst for accomplishment, and sallied forth on a quest to discover magic. Those quests led them *from* the city *into* the wilderness, *from* safety *into* danger, from normal, surface reality *into* realms of magic—Merlin's country. The knights may have lived in a literal, as well as metaphorical, city, but they recognized that magic lay outside the gates:

I came upon the enchanted vale,
down by the viaducts of my dreams.
Near Camelot hangs the tale of the enchanted vale.
In the upper room there the cup does stand.
In the upper room down by Avalon.

To better understand the transition that is taking

place in the story, we need to take a look at, of all things, the astrology of the times. This astrology is hidden away in the legends, but it wears a disguise. Sometimes it takes a sharp eye to find it.

In 1929, Katherine Maltwood wrote a book called *A Guide to Glastonbury's Temple of the Stars*. It caused an immediate stir because she claimed to have discovered, in the very face of the landscape which was, in her time, covered by fields and seemingly natural folds of the ground, a series of huge figures that were literally carved into the earth. In them she recognized the signs of the Zodiac; each figure constructed beneath its parent constellation.

At the time of her discovery, she was diligently at work illustrating *The High History of the Holy Graal*, a work that had been translated from old French by a Dr. Sebastian Evans. On the final page of that book, she found written these words:

The Latin from whence this History was drawn into Romance, was taken in the Isle of Avalon, in a holy house of religion that standeth at the head of the Moors Adventurous, there where King Arthur and Queen Guenievre lie.

Avalon? That was right there at Glastonbury! Could there be a connection between the Arthurian saga and astrology? In other words, could the saga itself, sometimes called *The Matter of Britain*, which was first spoken and later written down many hundreds of years later, contain an astrological message that duplicated the work of ancient Neolithic workers in stone? If so, it would illustrate a literary version of the now well-known and almost universal megalithic adage, "As above, so below."

This insight is worth the struggle to understand. We'll begin with two observations:

- First, as the earth spins on its axis, it wobbles a little bit. This wobble is called precession. What it means is this: Slowly, over the course of thousands of years, from the standpoint of any vantage point on earth the constellations appear to change places. Our present north star, Polaris, wasn't always located in the true north. (As a matter of fact, it still isn't, and won't be until the year 2100.)

- Second, as we have already seen, the dragon is an ancient symbol for earth energy, or what is now often called

"Pagan" religion, the spiritual viewpoint of Merlin the magician. Its sign in the Zodiac is the constellation Draco.

During much of the long span of millennia that encompassed the construction of the great stone monuments built all over western Europe and the British Isles—a vast amount of time that lasted from at least 4500-1500 BCE—there were actually two north stars, both located in the constellation Draco, the dragon.

In the time of the Arthurian legends, the dragon was a creature of the old, earth-centered, Pagan, belief system that derived its strength from the power of Mother Earth. It was later called, by Christian writers, the Devil, himself.

In megalithic times, the stars pointing to true north were already, at least from the standpoint of earth-bound astronomers, being "pushed out" of the way by the constellation later called in Welsh, and phonetically in Old Celtic, *Arth Vawr*. It means "Great Bear." Most western observers now recognize the principal stars of this grouping as the Big Dipper. In our time, the two stars forming the edge of the "dipper" point to Polaris, the modern north star.

Arth Vawr, transliterated into modern English, is, of course, Arthur. And who was Arthur's father? Who preceded the "Great Bear" himself? In the sagas, he is called Uthyr or Uther (which might mean either "Wonderful" or "Terrible") Pendragon, or "Head of the Dragon."

Think about this metaphorical relationship for a moment. In the popular telling of the story, what was a prime activity for Arthur (the Bear) and his knights, who succeeded Uther (the Dragon)? Slaying dragons, of course! This way of reading the story follows the old, old insight popularized by Sigmund Freud, that the son often goes about the business of usurping, or going beyond, his father. The Greeks played with this theme over and over again in their mythology. It is a common motif found in every culture on earth.

Thus it is that at precisely the same time in history that the megalithic stone structures across the western European countryside were being built, the North Stars, which had been in the constellation called Draco the Dragon, were being superseded by a single new star, pointed to by the constellation named for the Great Bear.

Much later, when it came time to tell the Arthurian stories, Arthur, the Great Bear himself, who was born a pagan but raised by Christians, was pushing out the Dragon—the old, pagan religion, while pointing to the new, victorious, pole star that now stood alone in the heavens. In this reading of the saga, the Church Triumphant, championed by both Arthur and his famous, pure-of-heart and dedicated Christian Knights of the Round Table, went about the countryside searching for Holy Grails and other religious artifacts, while Merlin, the part-Druid, part-Pagan, and generally mysterious magician of the old ways, who was secretly the power behind both Uther and Arthur, sadly slipped into his cave, just like Puff the Magic Dragon. He was the hinge upon which swung the historical gate marked "Pagan" on one side and "Christian" on the other.

When you understand the story in these terms, it makes perfect sense. History, after all, is written by the victors. In this case it was written by the Christian Church, which had a vested interest in putting to rest the old Dragon religions that pointed to the stars rather than Heaven, and derived its strength from Mother Earth instead of the Sun or, more appropriately, the Son, Jesus, the Christ. The time of the Dragon was dead. Long live the new age!

Let's sum up this transition from nature to city; from tribe to ego-centered individualism:

- Much of what we call civilization is an illusion—a thin veneer, floating on the surface of a much deeper reality. Beneath this so-called "civilized" veneer, painted by monks centuries ago, lies a deeply pagan system of belief that refuses to go away. The values of "Christian" Camelot were thus formed by pagan, shamanic, pre-Druidic formulations, that refuse to be compromised. They are with us still.

- When we read about Camelot, we experience a sea change in the Merlin story. Camelot is about transitions—from Paganism to Christianity, from nature to the city, from wildness to civilization, from magic to so-called rationality.

With the Christian king, Arthur, firmly ensconced on his throne in Camelot, with the transition from Pagan magic to Christian, civilized, ego-centered hierarchical values, now complete, it would seem as if the Merlin story could come to an end. It would be time for Merlin to echo the words of the *Nunc dimittis*, the Song of Simeon recorded in the second chapter of the *Gospel According to Luke*, "Lord, now lettest thou thy servant depart in peace according to thy word." The transition was accomplished. Civilization had defeated magic. Merlin's time was over.

But was it? There seems to be another chapter about to unfold. And perhaps it is the most important chapter in the entire saga.

The Text

Merlin, by Edwin Muir

O Merlin in your crystal cave
Deep in the diamond of the day,
Will there ever be a singer
Whose music will smooth away
The furrow drawn by Adam's finger
Across the meadow and the wave?
Or a runner who'll outrun
Man's long shadow driving on,
Burst through the gates of history, and hang the apple on
the tree?
Will your sorcery ever show
The sleeping bride shut in her bower,
The day wreathed in its mound of snow,
And time locked in his tower?

Chapter 9: Merlin and the Crystal Cave

Merlin in your crystal cave
Deep in the diamond of the day ...

Sometimes life may seem a little flat. Sometimes it may feel as if the magic is gone, replaced by a deadly technology that, though convenient, is certainly not very satisfying, much less exciting. During times such as those, it's good to remember that magic, like Merlin, never really dies. It has not departed from the world. It is merely sleeping in a crystal cave, deep below the surface of a humdrum life.

Such was the case with Merlin. According to the legends, he never died. He is, even as we speak, sleeping in a crystal cave, awaiting the time when Arthur, and the world, have need for him again. It's a wonderful image. But, let's face it, today's world has pretty much outgrown the idea of the kind of magic the Arthurian lore dishes up. Magic, at least Merlin's kind, seems a bit outmoded.

But is there substance behind the myth? Can we find a way to believe in real magic, given today's penchant for left-brain, analytical, scientific thinking?

Apparently so. There are a number of reputable scientists doing peer-reviewed research, using the tried-and-true scientific method, who are diving into the relatively new depths of quantum field research to discover some pretty counter-intuitive, mind-bending realities that seem to defy logic. Even Albert Einstein referred to the now-proven and accepted concept of quantum entanglement as "spooky." What earlier sages called "magic" is now readily accepted by down-to-earth, rational, scientists.

Let's spend a moment looking into a kind of reality that the early writers might have been referring to when they told stories of Merlin the "magician."

The kind of spiritual belief common in the time of Merlin was probably pretty close to what we now call Panpsychism. On the simplest level, Panpsychism makes the astounding claim that the universe, rather than being a sterile backdrop in which materialistic "stuff" evolves and develops, is instead a web of consciousness that brought about everything there is. This way of thinking is nothing new for those who follow metaphysics and some ancient religious systems. The equivalent idea of what is now often called the Akashic Field has been around for millennia.

But for scientists, operating within the parameters of mathematics and the scientific method, to give such a theory a name, and subject it to peer-reviewed papers, it is a breakthrough. What Panpsychism says is that the universe, just as it would have been understood in the time of the Merlin stories, might be self-aware.

For thousands of years, Zen masters have said that everything is one. But to give this concept official sounding labels such as "entanglement" and "proto-consciousness fields" is quite shocking. It means that lines of inquiry which have traditionally moved along two separate roads, called metaphysics and science, may have now merged into one superhighway.

Christof Kock, of the Allen Institute for Brain Science, a Seattle-based, independent, nonprofit medical research organization dedicated to accelerating the understanding of how the human brain works, has been designing experiments which define consciousness. His results indicate that biologic organisms are conscious if they are capable of changing their behavior when confronted by new situations. But if a system is able to act upon its own state and, in effect, determine its own fate, it is conscious, even if it is not biological or organic.

Although he has yet to present his ideas in the form of a formal "Theory of Mind," it is still a fascinating conjecture that has many theoretical physicists re-reading traditional religious systems of thought, and wondering if the ancients intuited what modern mathematicians have finally deduced. With more experimentation, Panpsychism might produce repeatable observations that could lead to fully-developed scientific theories about the nature of a universe that intentionally produced us. This is very close to how Merlin seems to have viewed his world. It might also help understand our unique place in a cosmos that has developed biological entities which are able to comprehend and become conscious of themselves as separate and individual beings, thus possessing egos.

To fully understand what this means, we first have to differentiate Panpsychism from other traditional systems of religious thought.

The first systematized religion, the belief system found in the Merlin sagas, was very probably what is now called *Animism*. This was the belief that everything is "animated" by fully-developed, conscious, and intelligent spirits that eventually came to be known as gods. This differs from Panpsychism in that panpsychists shy away from the idea that human-like, and especially God-like, attributes live within disparate objects found in nature. The distinction is important. When the ancient Greeks, for instance, wrote that "everything is alive," it sounds like Panpsychism. But they still viewed the universe as a stage upon which animated entities and objects played their part, rather than saying that the universe itself was the author of the play.

Pantheism came closer to the idea when it claimed that everything, collectively, is God. But it didn't go so far as to define the nature of mind and individual entities that make up creation. Baruch Spinoza, the great Jewish-Dutch Sephardic philosopher, considered God and the cosmos to be one, but didn't speak to the nature of mind itself, so some panpsychists claim him as their own and others don't.

The philosophical/religious system called *Panentheism* surmises that God penetrates everything.

According to this world view, a single, unified God is omnipresent as spirit in all things. But panpsychists argue that this doesn't really represent their views because the concept of "God within something" downplays the notion of the thing itself being a whole and unique expression of universal mind.

These distinctions are subtle. The average layperson probably thinks such semantics get in the way of understanding. But science is complex. To the true scientist/philosopher, specifics are important. If the basic, underlying concept of Panpsychism is that all things are an expression of a mind-like quality, or even that all things *possess* a mind-like quality, such minute differentiations are important.

The term Panpsychism was first invented back in the 16th century, after the time of the Merlin sagas, by Francesco Patrizi, an Italian philosopher. He combined two Greek words, *pan*, meaning "all," and *psyche*, meaning "mind," to describe his belief that all things have a mind-like quality. But this definition is so general in scope that it took until recently for scientists to employ it. What, after all, does "all things" mean? And what is "mind?" Are rocks, such as the stone that embraced Arthur's famous sword, conscious? Does an electron possess a mind? Until we can agree on definitions for those two concepts, further research is futile.

But Panpsychism moves the discussion away from objects and places it instead directly on the fabric of the universe itself. It is the cosmos that is mind, not the objects in it. They merely reflect the greater reality. Sir James Jeans, an English mathematician, astronomer, and physicist, perhaps said it best back in the 1940s: "The universe looks more and more like a great thought rather than a great machine."

It's important, however, to keep reminding ourselves that all this discussion about who first started thinking along the lines of Panpsychism detracts us from what is really important. The point is not that the modern theory of Panpsychism may not, indeed, be very modern. The point is that the theory has now bridged a great gulf that, until recently, separated science from philosophy, metaphysics, and religion. It is now officially a cross-discipline field of research. This is extremely important. It tells us that specialists from different academic disciplines are searching for the truth about our ancient origins, and that their research is beginning to converge.

Another way of saying this is that scientists are beginning to bring Merlin awake. They might be discovering, metaphorically speaking, that Merlin magic, now called quantum reality, still undergirds our civilized perception. He didn't disappear. He isn't dead. It's just that, after a suitable time, following his engineering the transition to the modern age, it is now possible to say that we are finally discovering a new, scientific language to describe what the old ones were saying in myth and legend.

If panpsychists can bring all things in both the material and the mental realm together under one roof, some startling conclusions come to light:

- "Mind" is inherent in all things. It is not injected into them or imposed upon them. They are expressions of mind itself.

- "Mind" has a focus to it. There is purpose and direction. The universe is not a cosmic accident. Its structure is not accidental, and its unity is real.

- The ancients were right when they intuitively grasped the fact that a forest, for instance, is not just a bunch of trees. It is an entity unto itself, with a unique personality or spirit. It consists of a multitude of systems, such as trees, plants, animals, rocks, and atmosphere. But together all these systems make up one bigger system. And forests are a part of a greater system called Mother Earth, which is part of an even greater system called the Milky Way galaxy, and so on, all the way up to a universe, which could very well be part of an even greater system called a Multiverse. In other words, everything is one. It is thus imbued with purpose and direction, because it is all an expression of Universal Mind.

Perhaps the easiest way to put this view in context is to reduce the whole problem to two distinct ways to view the universe—the view of those who first wrote about Merlin, and our predominately modern, academic view of the world. By doing so, we might discover they have more in common that first appears.

The *Panpsychism* view is that mind came before the universe, and that the universe is a self-realization, or manifestation, of that mind. "Mind" is, therefore, distinct from "brain." Our brains are receivers, not originators, of mind.

Think of a radio. Radio waves permeate our existence, but we're not aware of them until we tune into the correct frequency to pick up the signal. In this illustration, "mind" is the radio wave. "Brain" is the radio receiver. Merlin, therefore, is simply a highly developed radio receiver who was in tune with the spirituality of the cosmos.

The opposing view is called *Emergentism*. This is the view that a mindless universe came first, and mind somehow emerged from it at a later, unknown time. "Mind" is therefore a product of evolution. Chance rules the universe, and we are the lucky beneficiaries of that chance.

Emergence theory holds sway in the halls of academia these days. The problem is that it is very difficult to explain how mind managed to emerge in biological entities. Most physical attributes, such as eyes and ears, for instance, are simply genetic reconfigurations of things that existed before. Parents pass them on to their children. But mind isn't a biological constant. A human egg, as far as we can tell, doesn't have a mind. A newborn baby does. How and when does such a miracle take place?

In 2006, Galen Strawson wrote a ground-breaking article called *Realistic Monism: Why Physicalism Entails Panpsychism*. Not too many people read it, because it appeared only in *Oxford Scholarship Online*, but in it, he argued that there is one ultimate reality to the universe. "Mind" seems to be part of this ultimate reality. But "mind" consists of mental stuff, which cannot arise from non-mental stuff. Therefore, the one reality and "mind" must be identical. In his words, "Brute emergence is, by definition, a miracle every time it occurs." Given the universality of mind, that's a difficult fact to swallow, but Merlin would certainly have agreed.

From a strictly rational viewpoint, therefore, the concept of Panpsychism has to be at least entertained in any honest scientific/philosophical system of thought. If Strawson is correct, our ancestors seem to have anticipated modern scientific thought. What they *intuited*, with their right brain, we are *figuring out*, with our left.

Why is this important? Simply this:

We have to face the fact that it might be possible that those who wrote the sagas might have been on to something very real and important, but lacked the twenty-first-century language to explain it in words that we use today.

The world is a complex place. Sometimes we feel overwhelmed. It seems as though we are living insignificant, pointless lives that are bereft of meaning and purpose. But if we are a product of Universal Mind, that has been, so far at least, 13.8 billion years in the making, we matter. We are important! What seem to be significant political or religious divisions are, in the long run, pretty insignificant. If enough of us take the long view, we can rise above them and get about the important business of fulfilling our potential. And that's no small thing! It's exactly what the Merlin story is all about.

Panpsychism is, at root, about something that is very close to metaphysics, or twenty-first-century spirituality. It is not about religion, although many religious concepts have found their way into the discussion. It doesn't have a lot to say about theology, although theology may be important in the search for knowledge about the ultimate Mystery that is called God, Jehovah, Allah, Brahman, Manitou, the Great Spirit, Creator, the Ground of our Being, Eternal Consciousness, and many, many other names.

Instead, the scientific/philosophical study of Panpsychism is a search for that which is common to every human being who has ever lived, and who ever will live. Some people need to hear it in academic phraseology. Others need stories, such as the Merlin saga. But in the end, the message is the same.

Whether we consider our worldview to be sacred or secular, religious or humanist; whether we eagerly await the newest scientific discovery or spend our days dreading the next disclosure that might undermine our faith, we share something with every other human being on earth. We are alive. Vibrantly alive. Mysteriously alive. We live, and breathe, and swim, in an ocean of spirituality. We are not only one with Universal Mind, we are a product of it. We thus have immense value.

Think of the words great religions have used to describe spiritual attributes: compassion, goodness, love, joy, peace, everlasting life. Think of the ways the ancients linked spirit with the environment, and how indigenous peoples around the world see the handiwork of spirit in their surroundings. Ancients listened for the "music of the spheres," the song of the heavens. All we have to do is substitute the words "Universal Mind" for "Spirit," and we immediately enter into a common system of thought. Universal Mind is no longer pictured as a remote being "out there." It is now a universal construct "in here."

Maybe the time is now that Merlin is stirring, deep in his crystal cave, about to enter the world again. In a different guise, to be sure, but still Merlin!

His saga is about music, not spreadsheets. It is about understanding and compromise, not rules and regulations. It is poetry, not prose. But it can infuse spreadsheets, rules, regulations, and prose with meaning. In the end, what gives life purpose and makes it worth living is our universality and one-ness, the very essence of Panpsychism.

And that is our hope—that underneath it all lies Merlin, awaiting his return in our hour of need.

We're nearing the end of our journey. Let's once again summarize our findings:

- Another way of saying this is that scientists are beginning to bring Merlin awake. They might be discovering, metaphorically speaking, that Merlin magic, now called quantum reality, still undergirds our civilized perception. He didn't disappear. He isn't dead. It's just that, after a suitable time, following his engineering the transition to the modern age, it is now possible to say that we are finally discovering a new, scientific language to describe what the old ones were saying in myth and legend.

- We have to face the fact. It might be possible that those who wrote the sagas might have been on to something very real and important, but lacked the **twenty-first-century** language to explain it in words that we use today.

THE TEXT

From *The Life of Merlin* (*Vita Merlini*): Geoffrey of Monmouth
Translated by Translated by John Jay Parry
[1925, copyright not renewed]

I have brought this song to an end. Therefore, ye Britons, give a wreath to Geoffrey of Monmouth. He is indeed yours for once he sang of your battles and those of your chiefs, and he wrote a book called "The Deeds of the Britons" which are celebrated throughout the world.

Conclusion: The Return of Merlin

At the end of each chapter in this study, we have briefly summarized our findings. If we read them in order, they tell a compelling story. With a few editorial changes, minus the bold font and bulletpoints, this account marks the course of our findings:

Vortigern represents a person who is trying to bring order out of chaos for the wrong reasons. In the midst of a fragmented and vulnerable culture, he seeks personal power and prestige. He is the personification of ego run amuck.

Court magicians symbolize those insiders who follow traditional, institutional, hierarchical systems of government or religion, but have long since ceased to believe in them, other than using them as a means to an ego-centered end.

Saxons represent the intruding values of a materialistic culture that threaten the ethical and moral principles which underlie the very essence of what it means to be a spiritual human being.

The "strong tower" represents a moral, ethical place of security, in which we hope to shelter ourselves from the changing, swirling, shifting sands of cultural ambiguity.

Merlin represents the conjunction of matter and spirit, reality and illusion, magic and everyday life. He takes us beyond our normal existence, and reveals our dreams. He reminds us that there is more to life than normal experience, and offers hope to those forced to live in an increasingly sterile world.

The red and white dragons symbolize the presence of duality in the material world.

Magic is the exception, not the rule. It is always around us and ready to work its wonders, but we have to be alert to it or we'll miss it when it takes place. There comes a time when craft and skill are not sufficient. Only magic will do.

A spiritual force above and beyond duality is at work in the cosmos, and sometimes breaks through into human affairs. When it does, we call it magic. It isn't always pretty. There is a Middle Way that leads between the poles of all opposites to the place beyond, wherein are embraced all dualities.

We're never going to legislate a perfect civilization into existence. We can't moralize our way through to justice and peace. No scientific invention will usher in Utopia. To bring about those ends, sometimes we need the messy, confusing, counter-intuitive work of magic.

In this story we are witnessing a poetic version of the original split between the earth-based religion of the ancients, celebrated in oak groves and mountain sides, and the heaven-centered religion of the modern world, celebrated indoors with the latest technology. The split has only widened over time.

If we don't know who we are, how can we possibly act like we should? Underlying everything, hidden magic is the source of all that is!

We came to being and evolved within the energy of Mother Earth. Apart from her we cannot find our true essence. We need to slow down, quiet our heart, and learn to listen. That takes time and peace. Nothing short of that will do. In this sense, the ancients knew what we have forgotten. This is the central problem of the modern world.

Much of what we call civilization is an illusion—a thin veneer, floating on the surface of a much deeper reality. Beneath this so-called "civilized" veneer, painted by monks centuries ago, lies a deeply pagan system of belief that refuses to go away. The values of "Christian" Camelot were thus formed by pagan, shamanic, pre-Druidic formulations, that refuse to be compromised. They are with us still.

When we read about Camelot, we experience a sea change in the Merlin story. Camelot is about transitions—from Paganism to Christianity, from nature to the city, from wildness to civilization, from magic to so-called rationality.

Another way of saying this is that scientists are beginning to bring Merlin awake. They might be discovering, metaphorically speaking, that Merlin magic, now called quantum reality, still undergirds our civilized perception. He didn't disappear. He isn't dead. It's just that, after a suitable time, following his engineering the transition to the modern age, it is now possible to say that we are finally discovering a new, scientific language to describe what the old ones were saying in myth and legend.

We have to face a central fact. It might be possible that those who wrote the sagas might have been on to something very real and important, but lacked the twenty-first-century language to explain it in words that we use today.

Having now summarized the course of our exploration, it's time to draw some conclusions. The words of Geoffrey of Monmouth, taken from his *Vita Merlini, (The Life of Merlin)*, become especially significant:

I have brought this song to an end. Therefore, ye Britons, give a wreath to Geoffrey of Monmouth. He is indeed yours for once he sang of your battles and those of your chiefs, and he wrote a book called "The Deeds of the Britons" which are celebrated throughout the world.

Ego cannot be denied. It can only be controlled. The fact that we are born into this world with a sense of individuality curses us with the burden of ego, the sense that in some way we are different from everyone else. We might think that ego is found in our use of the words "I" and "my."

- "I" have a body.
- "I" have a mind.
- "I" have desires, hopes, and aspirations.

If this were, indeed, the case, we could say that ego and personal identity are the same thing. Thank goodness, however, this is not the case. We know it because we can also say "I" have an ego. Therefore, we understand that the individual known as "I" is somehow separate from ego, even though that seems, at first thought, a strange conclusion.

Perhaps, then, the essential, immutable "I" is closer to the word "soul" than ego. It's not exactly the same thing, because we can also say "I" have a soul. But if soul is eternal, existing before and after it takes on a body, a mind, desires, hopes, and aspirations, we can begin to think of ego as part and parcel of the whole package of being human. It is unavoidable.

Picture perfect unity, existing as truly one with everything there is. It would be completely at peace. There would be no conflicting duality, no troubling conflict. There would be no "I" and "you."

But there would also be no sense of individuality. There would be no real sense of purpose, of striving for something "more."

Back in the **Introduction** to this book we said this:

Think of it this way. Sometimes religion is not enough. We need more. Sometimes scientific explanations are insufficient. We need more. Sometimes mythological relevance doesn't quite satisfy. We need more. Sometimes psychological motivation doesn't do it for us. We need more. Sometimes philosophical discussion falls short. We need more. Merlin has become the "more."

If ego is part of what we must take on in order to experience the "more" of individuality, than, like all other functions of the body, it needs to be controlled. To be human is to experience the spectrum of emotions and forces that appear in the manifested realm of what we call reality, which, as we have seen, is, in a very real sense, an illusion. Our perception realm, as long as we are in the body, is subject to time. It is subject to heat and cold, sickness and health, love and hate, and all the other poles of duality. That may be the very reason we needed to take on physical life in the first place. None of these things can be experienced in a reality where all is peace and unity. And unless they are experienced, life in the Source of All That Is, the place of perfect unity, is not complete. To experience everything, Source needs to experience individuality. Only in individuality is there an experience of "I." But individuality comes with the blessing and curse of ego, a sense of self. And ego can desire both good and bad expressions of itself.

In that sense, we might safely say that each and every one of us is, in some sense, possessed by a "devil" and an "angel." But who is in control?

Sad to say, ego has immense power to deceive us into thinking that it is in control. Indeed, it has the power to convince us that ego *is* us—that it is the essential "I" that is experiencing all that goes on in our perception realm.

When this happens, when we start to identify with the negative power of ego, we really *are* demon possessed. We are egocentric. But ego is not eternal. It cannot experience life outside of individuality. It will never know perfect peace, perfect altruistic love, perfect stillness. Ego knows that when our bodies die, its life is over. Thus, it is terrified. If Hell is separation from "God," and by that term we refer to the perfect peace of unity, then Hell is ego's destination. That doesn't mean eternal punishment for "sins." It doesn't mean conscious torment in a place of fire and damnation. It means complete annihilation. Ego will simply cease to exist.

Yes—I "have" an ego. But the "I" who has an ego is capable of the power to keep ego in its proper place. Ego, present in all individuals, exists in a realm of duality—a place of choices. The "I" who has an ego is capable of choosing to follow its desires, for either good or bad.

That is what the story of Merlin is all about. According to this reading of the sagas, Merlin lived during a time of transition. Ego was ascending, seen metaphorically in the characters of Vortigern and the court magicians. For a while, as long as Merlin was still on the scene for a brief and shining moment, it seemed as though good was going to triumph in the person of young Arthur, his shining and pure Knights of the Round Table, and the splendor of Camelot. But ego can never be completely defeated. It lurks in the dark corners and recesses of the human experience. And as soon as it could, it reared its ugly head and brought the noble experiment crashing down.

Merlin, it seemed, may have been "more," but even *he* was not enough.

The good news, however, is that, in the end, this is a saga of hope. The better angels of our natures do not die. Merlin is not defeated. He merely sleeps in the crystal cave, awaiting the summons to awake and once more enter the fray.

Ego knows this well—so well that it seeks to keep the good news from us. Ego employs the toys, however dangerous, that power and greed have placed at its disposal. These are Ego's inventions, easy to manipulate to fulfill its desires.

There is nothing wrong with technology, such as it is. It can be used for good. But often, it is not. There is nothing wrong with the practice of politics and religion. Both can serve noble ends. But often they do not. There is nothing wrong with seeking individual gain. But if it comes at the expense of others, it serves only ego.

Ego easily turns into Narcissism. Narcissism is the worship of self—of Ego. Ego perverts the essential individuality of "I," turning it into a false god to be adored rather than a vehicle through which to experience the better side of duality. Perhaps this is why humans so often explore the idea of living forever in a material body. By doing so, we recognize the truth of annihilation that ego so fears.

So, Ego (notice, now, that we have begun to capitalize his name, signifying formal recognition of an actual entity) denigrates its archenemy. It calls it "magic." It seeks to destroy the essential truth of magic—the wildness, the unpredictability, the force that is capable of exploring unselfish, anti-egotistical, ways of dealing with the world.

But although history books seem to deny magic's presence, dealing up a continuous story of human wars and travesties, the Merlin sagas remind us that magic lives still, buried deep in the crystal caves of our psyches. He sleeps within every one of us. As does Arthur, the shining crown of our being, who is still present in our innermost being. Merlin's presence is revealed in art and music, in hundreds of myths that tell the story of the hero's journey, in dreams and visions that reveal the essential "more" we all crave.

We have the power to call him forth at any time. To each and every one of us he offers a magic sword, if we only choose to pull it forth from the ground of our being.

But that ground of being finds its true identity only in the Source from which we spring. Nature itself stands ready to heal us, to give us the strength to wield its power against an enemy who, we are assured, will never outlast us.

Ego may have deceived us into compromising Nature, its ultimate enemy. We may pierce Nature's heart with technologies invented by ego-driven corporate greed. We may crucify its body with nails of power, driven into its hands and feet. We may offer Nature as a sacrifice to ego's driven, twisted lust for its own perverted sense of "more," but the real "More" lies sleeping in his crystal cave, awaiting our summons. When we roll aside the stone that Ego has placed in front of the door of the cave, Merlin will come forth with a word of magical power. No longer will the word "more," be heard throughout the land. It will be replaced with the word "Enough." Merlin will be revealed in his full glory. No longer will humankind search for "more." It will find is has already experienced "enough."

Then, and only then, will Merlin's mission be accomplished. And we will be complete.

Further Reading

Bullfinch's Mythology. New York, NY: Gramercy Books, 1979

Campbell, Joseph with Bill Moyers. *The Power of Myth*. New York, NY: Bantam, Doubleday Dell Publishing Group, 1988.

Campbell, Joseph. *Transformations of Myth through Time*. New York, NY: Harper and Row, 1990.

Cotterell, Arthur and Rachel Storm. *The Ultimate Encyclopedia of Mythology*. China: Hermes House, 1999.

DeLaney, Gayle, PH.D. *All About Dreams*. SanFrancisco, CA: Harper Collins, 1993.

Gaskell, G. A. *Dictionary of all Scriptures and Myths*. New York, NY: Gramercy Books, 1981.

Gaskell, G. A. *Dictionary of all Scriptures and Myths*. New York, NY: Gramercy Books, 1981.

Hitching, Francis. *Earth Magic*. New York, NY: William Morrow and Company, Inc., 1977.

Houston, Jean. *The Hero and the Goddess*. New York, NY: Ballantine Books, 1992.

Ingerman, Sandra and Hank Wesselman. *Awakening to the Spirit World: The Shamanic Path of Direct Revelation.* Boulder, CO: Sounds True, Inc. 2011.

James, Simon. *The World of the Celts.* London, England: Thames and Hudson LTD, 1993.

Jones, Prudence and Nigel Pennick. *A History of Pagan Europe.* New York, NY: Routledge, 1995.

Kauffman, Stuart A. *Reinventing the Sacred: A New View of Science, Reason, and Religion.* Philadelphia, PA: Basic Books, 2008.

Keck, L. Robert. *Sacred Eyes.* Indianapolis, IN: Knowledge Systems, Inc. 1992.

Lacy, Norris J, editor, *The Arthurian Encyclopedia.* New York, NY: Peter Bedrick Books, 1986.

Macrone, Michael. *By Jove!: Brush Up Your Mythology.* New York, NY: Harper Collins, 1992

Malory, Sir Thomas. *Le Morte Darthur.* (Edited by R. M. Lumiansky) New York, NY: Collier Books, 1982.

Powell, Barry B. *Classical Myth.* Upper Saddle River, NJ: Prentiss Hall, 2001.

Radin, Dean. *The Conscious Universe: The Scientific Truth of Psychic Phenomena.* San Francisco, CA: Harper Collins, 1997.

Radin, Dean. *Entangled Minds.* New York, NY: Simon and Schuster, 2006.

Radin, Dean. *Supernormal: Science, Yoga and the Evidence for Extraordinary Abilities.* New York, NY: Random House, Inc. 2013.

Rolleston, T. W. *Myths & Legends of the Celtic Race.* London, England, The Ballantine Press.

Ross, T. Edward and Richard D. Wright. *The Divining Mind: A Guide to Dowsing and Self Awareness.* Rochester, VT: Destiny Books, 1990.

Sagan, Carl. *The Dragons of Eden.* New York, NY: Ballantine Books, 1977.

Starr, Kara. *Merlin's Journal of Time: The Camelot Adventure.* Solana Beach, CA: Ravenstarr Publications, 1989. New York, NY: Oxford University Press, 1989.

Stewart, Mary. *The Merlin Trilogy.* New York, NY: Harper Collins, 2004.

Van Renterghem, Tony. *When Santa Was a Shaman.* St. Paul, MN: Llewellyn

White, T.H. *The Once and Future King.* New York, NY: Berkley Publishing Company, 1958.

Willis, Jim. *The Dragon Awakes: Rediscovering Earth Energy in the Age of Science.* Daytona Beach, FL: Dragon Publishing Co., 2014.

Willis, Jim. *The Religion Book: Places, Prophets, Saints and Seers.* Detroit, MI: Visible Ink Press, 2004.

About the Author

The author of more than dozen books, ranging from ancient religion and 21st century spirituality to long-distance bicycle riding, he has been an ordained minister for over forty years, while working part-time as a carpenter, the host of his own drive-time radio show, an arts council director, and adjunct college professor in the fields of World Religions and Instrumental Music.

Other Books by Jim Willis

- Journey Home: The Inner Life of a Long-Distance Bicycle Rider
- The Religion Book: Places, Prophets, Saints, and Seers
- Armageddon Now: The End of the World A to Z
- Faith, Trust, & Belief: A Trilogy of the Spirit
- Snapshots and Visions: A View from the Now
- The Dragon Awakes: Rediscovering Earth Energy in the Age of Science
- Savannah: A Bicycle Journey Through Space and Time
- Lost Civilizations: The Secret Histories and Suppressed Technologies of the Ancients
- Ancient Gods: Lost Histories, Hidden truths, and the Conspiracy of Silence
- Supernatural Gods: Spiritual Mysteries, Psychic Experiences and Scientific Truths
- Hidden History: Ancient Aliens and the Suppressed Origins of Civilization
- The Quantum Akashic Field: A Guide to Out-of-Body Experiences for the Astral Traveler
- Censoring God: The History of the Lost Books
- Little Snow White: A Road Map for Our Time
- The Wizard in the Wood: A Tale of Mystery, Magic, and Meaning

See www.jimwillis.net for reviews and ordering details.

www.ingramcontent.com/pod-product-compliance
Lightning Source LLC
Chambersburg PA
CBHW071429070526
44578CB00001B/47